MW00390709

You have not experienced the full richness of tea's spiritual character until you have explored Frank Murphy's new book. To the reader, tea becomes more than taste, aroma, and fellowship. It is imbued with a quiet mystical quality that is rarely enjoyed in today's frantic world. Relax in a cozy corner with your favorite cup of tea and savor the serene beauty of Frank's inspired words. Indeed, through his insight a simple sip can become a portal to a new dimension filled with delight and wonder.

—Donald Wallis, Headmaster Emeritus, American Tea Masters Association

Tea is not just a beverage to Frank Murphy. It is more than an experience. The Spirit of Tea imbues Frank's soul. It is manifested through his writing in this book. Tea is part of him and he is part of tea.

—Pearl Dexter, Editor/Publisher *Tea A Magazine*®

THE SPIRIT OF TEA

THE SPIRIT OF TEA

Frank Hadley Murphy

Sherman Asher Publishing
Santa Fe

FIRST EDITION

ISBN: 1-890932-35-3
ISBN 13: 978-1-890932-35-0

Library of Congress Control Number: 2008925381

Design by Jim Mafchir
Edited by Cinny Green
Cover, title page and part title pages calligraphy by Joshua Hough
Drawings by Madison Cawein on pages 2, 20, 26, 34, 65, 66, 75, 88, 114,
plus spot drawings, and calligraphy on page 113
Drawings by Lee Murphy on pages 46, 82, 94, 108

Sherman Asher Publishing
P.O. Box 31725
Santa Fe, NM 87594-1725
www.shermanasher.com westernedge@santa-fe.net

Printed in Canada

For Li Po, who guided me across the desert
to the shores of a lake that lay beyond.

And for Lu Tung Pin, Lord of the Lake.

CONTENTS

FOREWORD

I met Frank Murphy some thirteen years ago. Frank had called me to ask about a tea that he was interested in purchasing, and just like that, we've been talking for thirteen years! I have to admit that Frank has been entirely too kind to me over these years, and has treated me with the utmost honor and respect that I am sure I don't deserve.

Recently, when Frank approached me to write the Foreword to his book, I was dumbfounded. I grew up in Hong Kong. Although Hong Kong was a British Colony during my boyhood days, English was not the first language of too many people. As a boy, I was one of the worst students in my entire school (at least to my teachers). I simply hated school and its many rules and confinements. Every day, I was out of my home early in the morning, destined to go toward what to me were hours of torture, but I was always able to find a few minutes of joy when I walked by the group of day laborers, a few of them gathered around a makeshift table and making "Gong Fu Tea" while they waited to be hired for the day. As a little boy, I had been fascinated by the way these people shared warmth and partnership during what must have been a very difficult circumstance, tied together by karma and tea. I would sit on the floor (and later be punished by my teacher for coming to school with dirty pants) or simply squat around with the men and watch. Once in a while, one of them would pass me their tiny Yixing teacup and I would take a small sip from it. The tea was bitter and strong, but my little mind never imagined that it could be any better or different in any way.

Some 45 years later, I am now the owner of Imperial Tea Court in San Francisco. The many, who have been attracted by what we are doing in this tiny tea company, give respect to the traditions of Tea and join in recognizing that fellowship begins with tea. From the beginning days thirteen years ago when I first started this adventure, we've grown into a three-store operation and are regarded by some as somewhat of a leader of traditional China tea in this country. Looking back to the days of the little boy sitting on the dirty sidewalk hoping to have a sip of tea, I've come a long way.

My friendship with Frank Murphy has quietly come a long way also. Frank has continuously referred to me as his teacher. Rather, I view myself as a messenger. I brought to Frank a spark that may have changed his life, just as those men long ago in Hong Kong changed mine. I shared many conversations with Frank, about family issues, business difficulties, responsibilities we shared together and with others. Frank has not only listened and responded with good advice always but also never missed a chance to gently cheer me on, not knowing how important those cheers are to me.

In this book, Frank Murphy has achieved a different level of tea unknown to me. Sparked by his own life's many events, Frank has found a connection to the mystic powers of tea and to the unknown and supernatural. In these levels of awareness, although I am a religious person, I must admit that Frank Murphy is far ahead of me and is, indeed, my teacher.

Roy Fong
San Francisco, California

ACKNOWLEDGMENTS

Friend and mentor, Roy Fong, owner of the Imperial Tea Court in San Francisco, whose wisdom, guidance, and direction, and tea continue to sustain my life. Thank you, Roy!

Donald Wallis, Headmaster Emeritus of the American Tea Masters Association, whose kindness and generosity embodied the essence of tea and initiated me, in rite and ritual, onto the path.

James Norwood Pratt, counselor, adviser, and friend, for welcoming me into the brotherhood and for the many cups we shared on Russian Hill and in China.

My editor, Eda Gordon, whose creative editorial insights brought this book to completion.

Pearl Dexter, editor of Tea A Magazine, for her encouragement and support these many years.

Stephen Bachelor, for providing me with all of the interviews he did with Korean monks and tea masters on behalf of John Blofeld.

Mary Alice Higby, proprietress of the Saint James Tea Room in Albuquerque, New Mexico, for introducing me to English tea in all its glory.

Jon Singer at the Joss Research Institute in Laurel, Maryland, for all botanical questions and for sharing his excitement and expertise as we drove through the Chinese countryside.

Fei-ju Beatrice Yang, Wen-ju Vivian Tsai, and Yi Shiu Liu of the Oolong Tea Square in Taiwan for introducing me to their Formosa oolongs. And Neng Tsz, for bringing us all together.

Eulalie Regan, librarian at the Vineyard Gazette, Edgartown, Massachusetts.

My tea sister, Marjana Tracy, with whom I have shared many extraordinary tea experiences.

Her husband, Madison Cawein IV, for his artwork and calligraphy.

Also for his artwork and friendship, my cousin, Lee Murphy.

Mark Sciscenti, the chocolate artisan, who supplied me with slabs of Valrohna and Scharfenberger from the divine trees of South America.

Camille Massie, who provided me with a yurt, firewood, and a tank of propane during extended retreats in the remote wilds of Glorietta, New Mexico.

Jon Oscher, for his generosity.

My wife, Anna, whose grace and beauty sustained me during many challenging moments.

I would also like to thank Donald Lamm, Louise Heydt, and David Riley, MD.

Finally, special thanks to Jim Mafchir of Sherman Asher Publishing and Cinny Green of THEMA.

INTRODUCTION

Most Americans' idea and experience of tea come filtered through England—black "milk and sugar tea" served in porcelain with a savory or two. England had the last word on tea, it seemed. At least this was how it was for me growing up in Massachusetts.

My earliest memories of having tea were with my mother. We would sit at the kitchen table on a summer evening and have tea with our dinner. She would take hers with lemon and sugar so that it retained its natural color, a color that reminded me of autumn, of gold.

After my mother died, a homeopathic physician recommended that I take the homeopathic remedy, Aurum Metallicum (potentized gold). It is prescribed for people who have just lost something or someone very valuable. It is also referred to affectionately as "homeopathic sunshine" because it brings light and warmth into the heart of a soul in loss. I benefited from the remedy, but what brought me greater comfort was tea, tea made in my mother's porcelain and served with lemon and sugar.

Ten miles from where my mother and I sat and had tea, and two hundred years earlier, there was another mom named Eunice Hillman who lived on a narrow dirt road. She was an elderly, infirm widow. Her notoriety centered on her desire for a pot of tea. Her hankering for tea came at a very inconvenient time because her fledgling country had just banned the stuff. So one day she asked her nephew, Captain Robert Hillman, who had a whaling sloop named *The Hannah*, to procure for her a chest of fine China tea when next he weighed anchor. Captain Hillman set sail for England; the year was 1774. When he returned, the patriotic local authorities found out about the contraband he'd smuggled in from England and they searched Eunice's house several times without success. The tea was in her barn. When things quieted down, Eunice invited her friends over and had a tea party. To this day, the road where Eunice lived, on the island of Martha's Vineyard, Massachusetts, is called Tea Lane.

It was China tea that Eunice had requested. It was China tea that was thrown into Boston Harbor, but it was not China tea that I grew up with. It was tea with names like Tetley, Twinings, and Salada. The first China tea I had was on December 31, 1993. On that day, I happened to find myself alone at home, with some time to spare. So I decided to make myself some tea. I had six little one ounce tins of tea my wife had brought me from her native San Francisco. It was a China tea sampler, and I decided to try the most exotic sounding of the lot. The name on the tin was Pou Nei.

I got a mug, put the loose leaves in a tea ball, and boiled some tap water. I remember I was standing at the kitchen sink when the tea was ready. I brought the mug to my lips and took a sip. The taste was unlike any tea I had ever had, and I became acutely aware that I had something very different in my body than I was used to. It wasn't just the taste of the tea that was unusual; it was what it was doing inside me. It was what I was experiencing in my body, my heart, and my soul that made me pay attention. I moved over to the kitchen table and sat down. And there I sat, letting the tea wash over me.

I began to track its movement through my body because I didn't want to miss a single thing that was going on. I followed the warmth of the fluid from my mouth down into my abdomen. In my belly there was the sensation of the tea spreading out onto the bottom of my pelvic floor. It then rose and pooled around my heart before it lifted into my head where it seemed, as the Chinese say, "to brighten my eyes." It was the calm and quiet that I noticed most, however, the poised, receptive state my body attained as I yielded to the tea. I remembered some words from *Mornings in Mexico* by D.H. Lawrence: "Something stood still in my heart and I started to attend."

I had an epiphany. Until that moment I had never had a direct experience of the divine through the plant kingdom. Now, here was this bush growing in the middle of my theology.

I was a seminarian at Sophia Divinity School in San Jose, California, at the time, so naturally, I was curious about what had happened. I went down to a local teashop and found a copy of a book called *The Tea Lover's Treasury* by James Norwood Pratt. I couldn't have been more fortunate. A master storyteller laid out the art and craft of tea before me. There were lots of leads to follow, teashops to track down, and new teas to explore.

Working off one of the tips from James Norwood Pratt's book, I contacted Mike Spillane at The G.S. Haley Company in California and asked if he could refer me to someone who could answer some questions I had about China tea. Mike gave me the names of two men who owned tea companies in the San Francisco Bay area. One of the men could not answer a single one of my questions; the other answered every one. It was at that moment I became a student of Roy Fong. So I began my study of tea, and I went out to San Francisco twice a year to learn from the elders of the American tea community.

This book is a compilation of my insights, observations, and experiences over a fourteen-year period—from formal and informal trainings and apprenticeships in the United States and in China, but most importantly, from making tea for myself in the privacy of my own home, sitting, sometimes for hours, in the ritual space I had created.

The teas I write about are all whole leaf, single estate teas, hand picked, hand fired, and hand finished on small farms. I procure them through Roy Fong's Imperial Tea Court in San Francisco's Chinatown. Roy travels to China several times a year and sometimes invites groups to accompany him. I have spent hours with him at China's National Tea Research Institute in Hangzhou and witnessed how well he is received and respected, whether he is working directly with farmers to recreate a tea that has been long forgotten or initiating a research project to produce an entirely new-tasting tea. Roy's approach is hands-on, in many cases overseeing the production of certain teas that require extra care and attention. Often the farmers are stretched and challenged by his rigid guidelines. The rewards of their intense labor and collaboration, however, inevitably bring a smile of pride and appreciation at tea-tasting time.

In 1994, Donald Wallis created The American Tea Masters Association (ATMA), focusing on the art of China tea. Each month members were treated to teas that Donald and Roy had designed themselves. They found that re-instituting old methods of tea manufacturing or supplementing current techniques produced the tastes and experiences they were looking for. The association's goal was to recreate the teas that were originally produced for the exclusive use of the emperors of China. These teas were the ultimate expression of the tea maker's craft; in other words, supreme examples of perfection in the art of tea. The ATMA also provided its members with a training program that took several years to complete. I was the first and only student to complete this course.

It was through the combined efforts of these men that Americans were first able to taste teas we had only heard about in legends or read about in books. Shortly after the Imperial Tea Court opened its doors on July 4th, 1993, Donald and Roy procured from China's National Tea Research Institute, for the very first time, the top 100 teas that won the National Tea Competition that year. (The English translation of those teas follows in chapter four, The Cast of Characters.) Donald and Roy have also sponsored several Chinese and worldwide tea competitions in which I had the honor to participate.

The setting for my formal studies of tea was created by Donald Wallis at his Jade Brook Tea House on Leavenworth Street in San Francisco. When Donald carefully closed the 400-pound lead door of Jade Brook behind me, I felt sealed in. Donald had constructed a rarified environment. The exquisite beauty of the Tea House both refined my senses and softened my soul. As I relaxed into the soft lighting and soothing pastels of the décor, I would watch Donald prepare the teas of the day with impeccable and meticulous attentiveness.

The course included a number of "intensives" that covered a wide range of study, including: tea cultivation, harvesting, and processing; tea botany and leaf chemistry; brewing techniques in traditional and non-traditional settings; tea history, art, and spirituality; as well as endless side-by-side taste test comparisons of hundreds of teas. It provided an opportunity to sample a vast array of teas from China's National Tea Competitions. These "intensives" lasted for five days straight. At the end of each ten-hour stretch, Donald would "break the seal" on that door and I would step out into a balmy San Francisco evening. Sometimes after Jade Brook, I would hike over to Russian Hill and have dinner with James Norwood Pratt, who wasn't difficult to find after I read his book. He also had a tea concern affiliated with Roy Fong called JNP Tea Luxuries, and he lived "right up the hill" from the Imperial Tea Court.

Norwood always considered himself a student of Roy Fong's and eventually we both became Roy's "senior students," as Norwood put it. In the year 2000, the Year of the Dragon, we all traveled to China together, wandering from one tea adventure to another. We did a two-week tea intensive in the field with Roy and members of ATMA.

While these three men were my mentors, counselors, and advisors, it was really tea itself that initiated me. As my studies deepened, so did the epiphanies, and I began to feel I was probing into the very nature of the universe.

So moved was I by some of my experiences with tea that I had the desire to become a tea advocate. I wanted to dispel the many inaccuracies that continue to be perpetuated by members of the American tea community, like the myths of a dysfunctional family. I also thought of starting a plants' rights movement concerned with the preservation of the species, and educating people that plants are as sentient as we are. At other times, I imagined a new mythology surrounding this "Queen of the Camellias," to take the romance and mysteries of tea to a new level.

Each book I read, each lecture I attended had a piece of the puzzle. Each had gems to share, but nothing seemed to address what I had encountered from my first sip of tea. There came a time when I reached a saturation point in my tea education, when I had to put down everyone else's books and draw back into the richness and depth of my own experience. I had to go back to those places where my heart first opened. This book is a testament to those moments.

I am grateful to be able to share this book with you. For me, it is as if I have been given the opportunity to sit down with you and make tea for you myself. It is my hope that this book, like tea, will provide a little balm to soothe the soul.

Frank Hadley Murphy
Santa Fe, New Mexico
January 6, 2007

THE SPIRIT OF TEA

茶

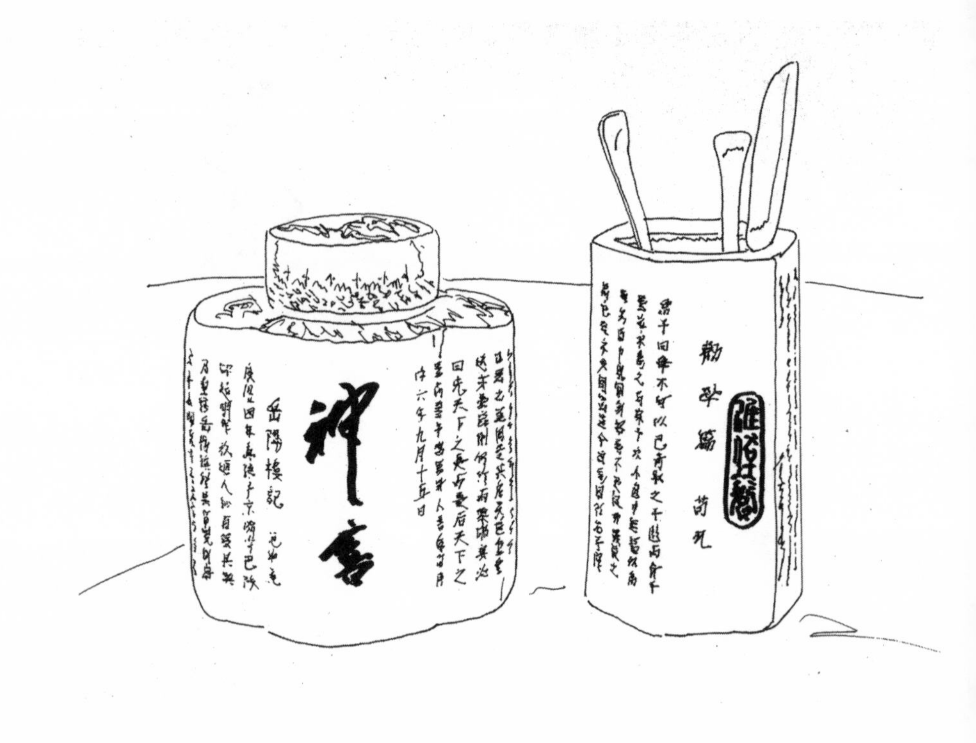

I

THE SPIRIT OF TEA

The deepest mysteries are found without any teaching.
—*I Ching*

CREATION SPEAKS TO US through all its manifestations, if we are willing to listen. Science may be able to quantify tea's effects on our bodies but it cannot quantify its effects on our souls, and that's exactly where tea shares with us her deepest mysteries.

Her sobering humility resonates with our own original nature.

Her subtle beauty reminds us of the beauty of our own perfection.

Her soothing calm cuts through our spiritual materialism and brings us to a state of grace.

She wakens in us not only the intellect of the mind but more importantly, the intelligence of the heart.

Tea calls to our deepest selves and invites us to celebrate with it.

Any plant that can do all of these things must have an element of holiness about it. You may think that this is a lot for a plant to do. You may think that I imbue tea with charms it does not possess. You are not alone. The Buddhist scholar and writer, John Blofeld, felt the same way. After reading a number of interviews with Korean monks and tea masters about their experiences with tea, Mr. Blofeld wrote in his *Chinese Art of Tea*: "This is too much! The virtues these people claim for tea are disproportionate!"

The only thing that is disproportionate, I believe, is how far we have drifted from ourselves and from our brothers and sisters in the plant kingdom. Tea asks us to listen. Some teas require from us not only a quiet palate but also a quiet space in which to partake of them. With tea, we can create for ourselves a nurturing, receptive environment, an altered space of calm and reverie. Into this space, as if invoked, can step insights, intuitions, sensations, and premonitions that we may not expect.

The Japanese gentleman, Kakuzo Okakura, was so impressed by his experiences with tea that he reverently wrote in his book *The Book of Tea*: "Why not consecrate ourselves to this Queen of the Camellias and revel in the warm stream of sympathy that flows from her altar?" He continued, "When we consider how small after all the cup of human enjoyment is, how soon overflowed with tears, how easily drained to the dregs in our quenchless thirst for infinity, we shall not blame ourselves for making so much of the tea cup."

Tea has been used in eastern religious rites and rituals for hundreds and hundreds of years. It has always fascinated me that easterners chose tea, a stimulating beverage, to use in their sacramental offerings and that westerners chose wine, a depressant. While a priest is said to transubstantiate bread and wine into the body and blood of Christ, tea can transubstantiate us. It can transport us and transfix us at the same time, and that I call rapture.

Like all plants, tea predates man and may have something to teach us about our own survival. The scripture of the earth is imprinted upon every leaf. What that scripture is, is left to us to discern as individuals. All plants blossom and set fruit to some degree. But plants, as sentient beings, can blossom and set fruit a second time in the fertile soil of our hearts. This is their greatest gift to us.

Perhaps there is
Inscribed upon the leaf
A sutra of its own.

Sometimes I wonder if what appears as steam rolling off the surface of my cup is not really the individual soul of each leaf rising heavenward. Sprinkling a little water over your tea leaves before you brew them awakens them from their slumber, but we may awaken them further with prayer. Call upon the soul of the species. Invoke the devas of the tree. Enlist their aid. They are there to help us.

Once, as I prayed over the leaves, holding my hand aloft in a final gesture of blessing and thanks, I watched the field open to reveal the clear red liquor of the tea. To my amazement, three white cranes emerged from the bubbles around the edge of the glass. Before they could reach the far side of the glass, two lifted off and disappeared into the steam rising up to heaven; the other dove down into the leaves below. I kept watch over my brew. Some leaves sailed to the surface while others receded, exploding into clouds of downy hairs. As I drank this tea in the still silence around me, the cranes returned—two from heaven and the other from below the surface of the lake. No wonder this tea retrieves my soul, I mused, when cranes fly in from Yunnan and bring with them gifts from the mother trees.

If you're a little self-conscious about praying over your tea in the morning, remember: spiritualizing tea changes its leaf chemistry. Why not offer a little comfort of your own to these leaves as they yawn and stretch out in the vessel before you? It is the least you can do to honor them. They are, after all, offering up the last bit of their lives to us, plucked as they were, at youth, from the bush.

Though dictionaries and encyclopedias insist that tea is a bush, in its wild and native habitat, it is a *tree*. All you have to do is look off to the sides of the tea gardens and there they are: tea trees ten to forty feet high! Tea is a tree kept, against its nature, at shrub level for easy harvesting. Were it not grown as a bush, we would not have tea; there would not be that intense concentration of the goddess Thea's essence in the leaves. The amazing thing about tea is she shares with us her desire to fulfill herself as a tree. This is why we can have such expansive experiences, as if we were being lifted up into the branches of a tree. Or such grounding experiences, where we feel as if we were being brought down into the roots of a tree.

Tea makes a tremendous sacrifice bowing to the demands of

human cultivation. Still she graciously yields her bounty, her wisdom. It is when we bow back to her that tea becomes a sacrament.

There are no words of restraint in the prose and poetry of tea, nor in the writings of connoisseurs and tea masters. Listen to these words by Kakuzo Okakura: "In the liquid amber within the ivory porcelain, the initiated may touch the sweet reticence of Confucius, the piquancy of Lao Tzu, and the ethereal aroma of Sakyamuni himself."

You may cynically ask, what kind of tea was this guy drinking? But some of you may recall *The Remembrance of Things Past* by the French writer, Marcel Proust:

> And soon, mechanically, dispirited after a dreary day with the prospect of a depressing morrow, I raised to my lips a spoonful of the tea in which I had placed a morsel of the cake. No sooner had the warm liquid, and the crumbs with it, touched my palate than a shudder ran through my whole body, and I stopped, intent upon the extraordinary changes that were taking place. An exquisite pleasure had invaded my senses, but individual, detached, with no suggestion of its origin. And at once the vicissitudes of life had become indifferent to me, its disasters innocuous, its brevity illusory. This new sensation having had on me the effect which love has of filling me with a precious essence; or rather this essence was not in me, it was myself. I had ceased to feel mediocre, accidental, mortal. Whence could it have come to me, this all-powerful joy? I was conscious that it was connected with the taste of the tea and cake, but that it infinitely transcended those savors, could not, indeed, be of the same nature as theirs. Whence did it come? How could I seize upon and define it? (Marcel Proust, *Remembrance of Things Past, Volume 1: Swann's Way and Within a Budding Grove* [New York: Random House, 1981], 48)

As we read about man's various encounters with tea over the centuries, we realize that there is a feminine presence dominating the leaf. China tea lore is rife with tales of fairies, sprites, and goddesses. In his book *Chinese Tea Culture*, Wang Ling writes: "However, in the legends about tea there is more a flavor of fairies than of Buddhism. Fairies impress the Chinese people more than Buddhism does, for fairies, who are alive, stand for beauty and wisdom, qualities which are pursued by the Chinese people, especially laborers."

Whether addressed as the Goddess of all Herbs or Queen of the Camellias, the soft and soothing graces of the greens, green teas particularly, disarm us and bring us peace.

At first I was disappointed when I learned tea's botanical name was changed from *Thea* to *Camellia*, in honor of botanist Georg Josef Kamel (1661–1706) because Kamel is German for the Latin name *Camellia*. It felt like a slap in the face of the eternal feminine by the ruling patriarchy, taking the honor away from a goddess and giving it to a Jesuit missionary. When I thought about it, though, I realized Camellia isn't such a bad name for tea, considering that the feminine name Camille or Camilla means "noble youth assisting at religious rites." Yet Thea is a much more evocative and romantic name, more in keeping with tea's colorful mythology and history. The name Thea also fits as a goddess of light and luminaries, because that is exactly what tea does. She illuminates our souls.

Some days when I'm struggling through what seems like the dark and heavily forested regions of my psyche, a cup of tea will graciously bring me to a sunny little knoll with a view. I feel the warmth of the sun on my back and my whole body relaxes as I yield to the spirit of tea.

11

THUNDER IN THE MIDDLE OF THE LAKE

Both tea and the I Ching are ancient vehicles in Chinese culture and present "a way" unto themselves.

IN 1974 I WAS LIVING in Milton, Massachusetts, a few blocks from the Museum of American China Trade. Unbeknownst to me, the museum's associate director, Francis Ross Carpenter, was just finishing up his translation of Lu Yu's *The Classic of Tea*, or the *Cha Ching*. A local publishing house in Boston, Little, Brown and Company, released *The Classic of Tea* that year. It is the only translation we have of Lu Yu's book.

Lu Yu, whom many consider to have been China's patron saint of tea, lived during the Tang dynasty (618–907 AD). His book was published around 780 A.D. It was the definitive edition on tea at the time. It was so comprehensive that the Chinese saw no reason to say anything further about tea for a long time to come. Reading Lu Yu's book reveals the profound impact tea had upon his life. But there was another powerful influence—a book that predated him by over a thousand years—the *I Ching*, or the *Book of Changes*.

It was also in 1974 that I bought my first copy of the *I Ching*. This ancient book of Taoist oracles contains eight trigrams. (A trigram is comprised of three lines.) When these eight trigrams are combined with one another they create 64 hexagrams. A hexagram, then, is a stack of six lines that starts at the bottom and builds up, comprising two trigrams, a lower one and an upper one.

Some of the lines are solid, some broken, some about to change into a broken line and others about to form a solid line. There are many active forces at work within these hexagrams because the trigrams are constantly shifting and interacting with each other. Thus the name, *Book of Changes*.

TEA AND THE I CHING

In his introduction to Lu Yu's *The Classic of Tea*, translator Mr. Francis Ross Carpenter writes that Lu Yu's name was "closely bound to that most venerated of China's early classics, the *Book of Changes* known also as the *I Ching*." In addition to the name Lu Yu, his style or fancy name was Hung Chien ("the wild goose advances"). It would seem that he took both names himself after divining one day with the aid of the *I Ching* and drawing hexagram #43, *Chien*, or "gradual advance." The hexagram said: "The wild goose (*hung*) gradually advances (*chien*) to the great heights (*lu*). Its feathers (*yu*) can be used as ornaments." Other books suggest the abbot of a Chan Buddhist monastery where Lu lived as a youth divined Lu Yu's name for him from the *I Ching*. Whatever the story, it is clear that Lu Yu was intimate with the *I Ching* and even embellished his brazier with three trigrams from the text. Those three trigrams were *kan* for water, *li* for fire, and *sun* for wind. In *The Japanese Way of Tea*, Sen Soshitsu XV writes:

> This adornment allows one to see clearly Lu Yu's attitude as he prepared tea. He was not merely brewing a beverage for drinking, for in making the tea there was a spiritual dimension. As he boiled the water, he invoked the spirits that controlled the wind and those that controlled the fire and water. The tea itself became a kind of offering. This attitude demonstrates, therefore, that in terms of his underlying approach to tea, Lu Yu was determined to plumb to the heart of nature in each cup.

Tea brings all five elements of Taoism into play: water, fire, earth, wood, and metal. Lu Yu felt the mere act of drinking tea balanced the five elements in our bodies. Some teas do just that.

Of all the hexagrams of the *I Ching*, the one I return to again and again is hexagram #17, *Sui*, or following, where the image reads, "Thunder in the middle of the lake." The lower trigram is *Chen*, which means "arousing thunder," and the upper trigram is *Tui*, "the joyous lake." This is the hexagram that best captures the essence of tea. Tea represents the rousing, mobilizing force of thunder resting within the gentle and joyous waters of the lake.

In another translation of the *I Ching*, by Stephen Karcher, we read that this hexagram "shows an outer stimulus rousing inner energy." *Tui*, the lake, may be considered a container full of water, much like a brewing vessel. And within this vessel, this lake, is an elixir that both mobilizes and gladdens. The calm, reflective waters of the lake still our busy minds and the arousing nature of thunder awakens our hearts.

As the *I Ching* says: "Of all the forces that move things, there is none more swift than thunder," and "Of all the forces that give joy to things, there is none more gladdening than the lake." The *I Ching* also tells us: "All things come forth in the sign of the arousing."

Tea is all of these things.

Going deeper, the book also says that the lower trigram *Chen* signals "the shock that comes from the manifestation of God within the depths of the earth." Here, of course, it would be within the depths of the lake.

The animal that symbolizes *Chen* is the dragon. The Chinese believe that dragons inhabit all bodies of water. It is from the dragon that thunder and lightning issue, especially as the dragon rises up out of its watery abode into stormy skies. It is the sound of thunder from the dragon that wakens the seeds of the old year, whether in the ground or in our hearts. The rising dragon also brings the rains, nourishing the earth with soft and fertilizing showers.

Dragon energy is equated with kundalini energy rising, pushing upward from the base of the spine. The trigrams *Chen* and *Tui* also have natural tendencies to rise upward. Tea can also mobilize the *chi*, or *qi* (vital energy or breath) in our bodies and cause it to rise in us, clearing blocked meridians as it goes. As we partake, our life force is wakened from below and rises up, flowering in our hearts, minds, and souls. It is so appropriate that this hexagram should provide a refuge for the dragon's domain.

Hexagram #17 is also the hexagram of the autumn months, when the arousing thunder with its attendant lightning, or electricity, withdraws into the earth to begin its winter rest. The Chinese once believed that thunder came from the earth. Rather, it is into bodies of water that the thunder retreats. Tea, too, flowers and sets fruit in the fall, then "withdraws into the earth," lying dormant through the winter. If there were an "autumn" in our day, it would be when we took tea at the end of the day, when we "go inside for rest and recuperation," as hexagram #17 advises.

AUTUMN FLOWER TEA
I have tried to apprehend you, sweet November
But your moons bestow both joyousness and grief
And now you send an ally from September
To aid my apprehension through the leaf.

In my cup I watch the flowers steeping,
Angels rising slowly from the earth.
And in my heart I know that I am keeping
Vigil in these months before my birth.

One sip and all I need remember,
A message from neither outside nor above:
These leaves picked nine days into September,
The calming centralizing ground of love.

Though the waters of the lake are still, they are not stagnant. The life force of the arousing dragon within the lake is forever vibrant and dynamic. The waters of the brewing cup may be still, but clouds of downy hairs rise up beneath the surface. The wisdom of the dragon whispers through our tea. We simply need a sip to share in its mysteries.

When I first heard the call of the dragon, it came from beneath the waters of the lake, *Tui*, the joyous water of my soul. In Karcher's *I Ching*, he describes *Tui* as "the Joyous Dancer, the spirit of open water.... She dances with the *shen* and feels the spirit in her body and gives it words." *Tui* represents the sorceress or "the woman who speaks." The goddess of tea, Thea, is the woman who brings light when she speaks.

The judgment guiding this hexagram is *Sui*, or following. The attribute of the upper trigram, *Tui*, is joy or gladness. The attribute of the lower trigram, *Chen*, is movement. "Joy in movement induces following." I welcome into my body the young and feminine presence of a tea and I follow her movement, her passage, within me. I feel where she invites me to yield and I also feel where I may resist her invocations.

YIN AND YANG TEAS

In chapter four, The Cast of Characters, you will see that there are six traditional categories of tea: White teas, Yellow teas, Green teas, Oolong teas, Black teas (or Red in China), and Puerh teas. I have been developing another way to classify tea, a system that takes into account tea's effect on our bodies. In my approach there are only two categories: those teas with character traits that are either *yin* or *yang*.

Yin and yang describe two complementary principles of traditional Chinese philosophy and medicine. In simple terms, they are dark (yin) and light (yang) in constant motion, and all things in nature have yin and yang states. The yin teas, represented by the upper trigram *Kun*, the receptive earth, move downward. The yang teas, represented by the lower trigram *Chien*, the creative heaven, move upward. In all hexagrams the two central lines symbolize humanity. The bottom two lines represent the earth and the upper two represent heaven. Their influences converge in the heart and bring peace.

The yin teas are the whites, yellows, greens, and some of the oolongs—teas that are soft, feminine, yielding. The yang teas are more masculine, starting with the oolongs, and encompassing the blacks and Puerhs. These teas are assertive, bolder, and more declarative.

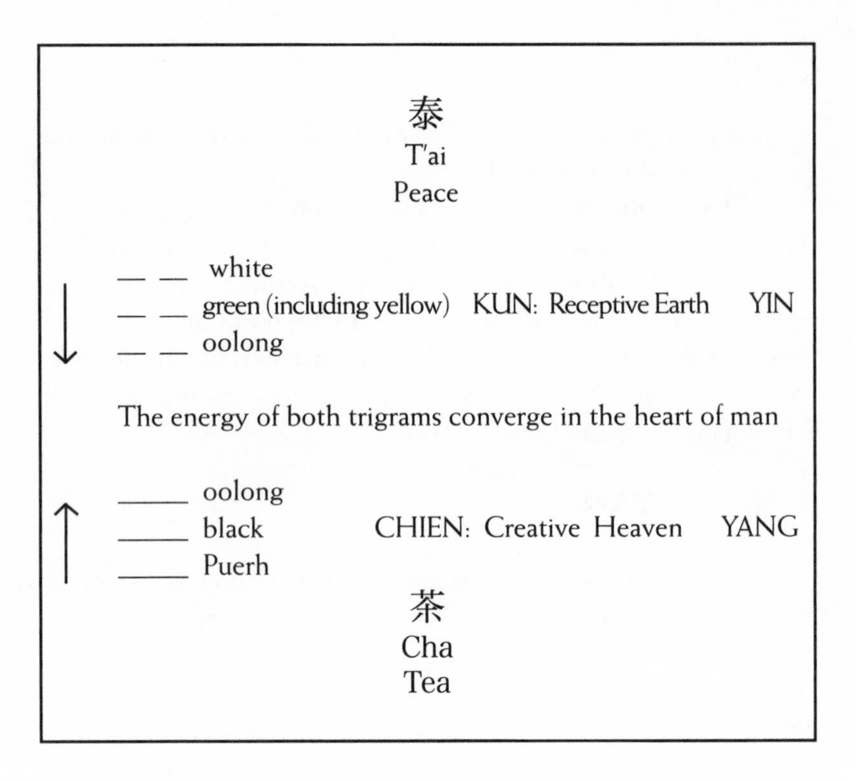

All tea takes you into the trunk of the bush. The yang teas, being expansive and light bearing, can bring you up into the sun through the branches. The dark and feminine yin teas can bring you down the trunk into the earth through the root system. While the yangs present expansive sensations and the yins present contractive ones, there are no laws that govern each tea. We may journey in either direction.

We can rise up through the branches of the bush into heaven and lose ourselves and we can also "disappear" by dropping down through the roots and out of the bottoms of our feet. Sometimes it is important to pull ourselves back down from these celestial realms, and conversely, to abandon our flirtation with the earthly depths so that we do not wander too far astray. Hooking up (reacquainting) one end with the other creates a cycle within which we may move our energy and stay grounded at the same time.

On an energetic plane, the yin teas cannot only bring us into our bodies but take us deep down inside. In contrast, the yang teas can lift us up into an expanding universe where we feel we are blossoming, flowering from our hearts right up to the top of our heads.

Of all the gifts that tea has brought me, joy is the most enduring. Of all the forces that tea has awakened in me, none is more vital than the creative, mobilizing spark of life: the thunder in the middle of the lake.

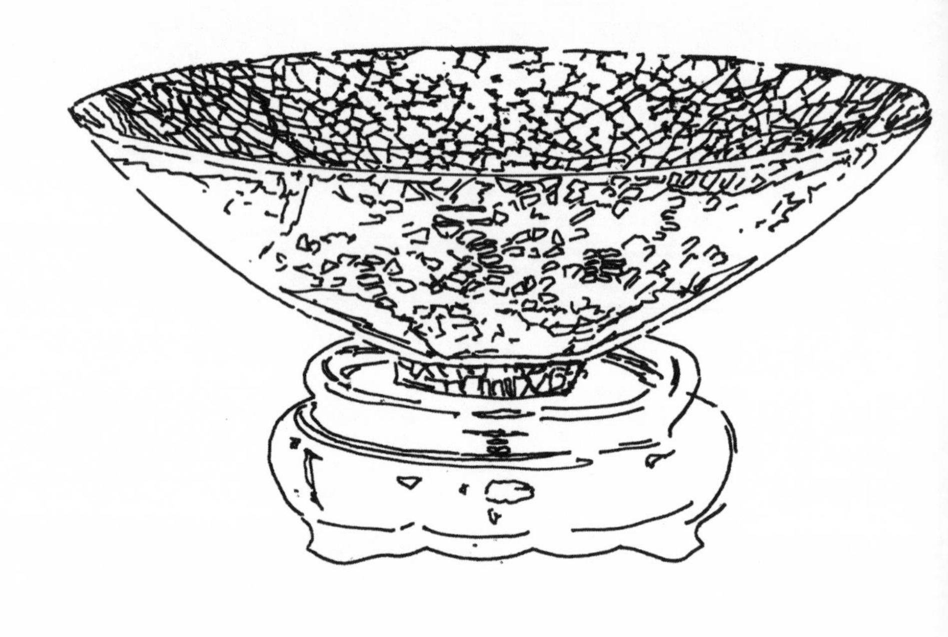

III

EVERYTHING I NEED TO KNOW IS IN THE CUP

If you cannot find the truth right where you are,
then where do you expect to travel in search of it?
—*Dogen*

I GET SO BUSY SOMETIMES that I feel I am crowding myself out into the margins of my day. The ritual of tea returns me to the center of the page. But rituals require constant adaptation, or else they risk degenerating into something stagnant, empty, and meaningless. If you over-focus on technique, rather than on the tea, your heart will not be in it.

What calls me to tea each day is different, but the moment I begin to yield to that desire, things start to shift. My mood softens and I become more animated because I know that I will be tending to myself in a soulful manner.

Tea is a vehicle through which I experience the divine. It is not difficult for me to classify this experience as a *sacrament* when dictionaries define sacrament as a testament to inner grace or as a channel that mediates grace. Any experience, for that matter, that brings me to a place of inner calm, allowing my heart to open and my body to hear that still small voice within, is a sacramental experience.

One aspect of tea's mystical nature is its ability to bring us to places of beauty within our souls. What more could we ask of a friend? Beauty softens our hearts and makes us more attentive to the voices of the soul. This amazing gift is a kind of blessing, as any opening of the heart is a blessing. Perhaps that is why the word *beauty* and the word *beatify*, or to bless, share the same root stem.

I begin my tea ritual by clearing a space in the middle of my day where I may give myself over exclusively to the act of making tea. The ritual is, by its very nature, a meditation practice. The space I am engaged in creating requires that I be intent upon my task, with a clear and undivided mind. I have to be mindful of what I am doing or I will chip the porcelain, or worse, destroy the tea.

I then gather about me the equipage, objects of great beauty and value I will use in making the tea. I place them on a white tea towel, to see the contrasting colors of the tea as it infuses. Whether a sterling creamer or a jade gaiwan, preparing tea with elegant things elevates the experience and sets it apart. Like water, it is tea's nature to flow into the spaces that have been created for it, whether that space is the patient pot before us or the chambers of our heart.

I do not feel I can meet tea empty handed and expect her to respond. The noble qualities I intend to coax from the leaf I also ask of myself. So I create the atmosphere necessary to meet this divine herb with reverence and respect. If I cannot have tea in an honorable way, I do not have it at all. Even after a thirty-day abstinence, it may take another five days to create the proper space within which to have tea. Some teas may ask for a period of fasting or cleansing before you brew them. Or, it may be as simple as taking a few moments to clear your mind.

You see, I'm already setting myself up for something to happen, before I've even had my tea.

I then ask myself, as a friend does, what tea shall I invite into my space today? Perhaps I already know what tea I want. Perhaps I dreamed about it the night before or smelled it on a morning breeze.

I like watching water as it heats up so I use a small open saucepan. For years, I had the habit of clipping a thermometer on to the side of my pan. It was a time when I was drinking a lot of green tea. Some of them were quite finicky! Some, like a two-week-old Lion's Peak Lotus Heart Dragon Well, required 55 degrees Celsius for 50 seconds. Others were more versatile at 60 to 70 degrees. After years of gazing mindlessly into my saucepan waiting for the water to warm, I began to get a pretty good idea what the water looked like at 60 degrees Celsius. If you're prone to using an electric tea kettle, however, it's easy to tell what the water's doing by the sound or by feeling the outside of the kettle itself if you're just heating the water up gently.

Here in Santa Fe, I hear complaints from the English tea-drinking community that they can never get their water hot enough. It's true. Santa Fe is 7,000 feet above sea level and water doesn't boil here at 212 degrees Fahrenheit. It boils at about 196–198 degrees. This may not be hot enough to extract certain flavors from blended black teas that are designed for boiling water. If you are determined to get the water hotter you may want to leave it on the stove for a while at a full rolling boil. Or, you can "nuke it" in a microwave. Both methods may raise the temperature two degrees or more. Throwing Puerh leaves into microwaved water at sea level can be very dramatic. It will fizzle, froth, and foam over. It will also look and taste different.

When the water gets to its desired temperature, I pour some into the brewing vessel to warm it up. I then transfer that water to the container I will be drinking from to warm it up as well. Most people would then throw this water out, but here in the desert water is precious. What I do is retain this water in a separate basin to water plants with later.

It is not a good idea to pour this "warming water" back into the saucepan because it will offset the chi of the remaining water. Similarly, it is disruptive to lift the lid off of a teakettle, remove a cover from a teapot, or stir brewing leaves prematurely. All of these disruptions can disturb the chi you have created, throwing it off balance.

I place dry tea leaves in the warmed brewing vessel with a wooden spoon. I am careful not to use a metal spoon because in Taoism wood and metal oppose each other; their energies conflict. Trees have adverse memories of metal—the desecration by axes, saws, and nails. For that reason, I line metal tins with paper.

To invoke the fragrance of the tea, I then sprinkle a few drops of heated water over the leaves. I bring these moistened leaves to my nose and inhale. I may linger here for several seconds breathing in the wonderful aromas the leaves exude.

DEFUSE WHILE YOU INFUSE

I put the vessel down on the counter and pour water in for the first infusion. This is the point some call "the agony of the leaves." Helen Gustafson describes it well in her book by the same name: "This phrase refers to the writhing, swirling action of the loose leaves immersed in boiling water. (The leaves may appear tormented and miserable, like autumn leaves in a storm, but they may also look dancing and fanciful; perhaps the coiner of this famous phrase was dyspeptic that day.)" Right on, Helen! I, too, felt whoever projected this feeling into the leaves must have been having a difficult day.

I could never relate to the use of this phrase at this particular point because I have always felt that tea rejoices in its reunion with water. If there were any pain or agony in the life of a tea leaf, it would most likely be at the point when the leaf is first separated from its mother, when it is first plucked or torn from the bush. Another moment of agony might be when the freshly picked leaves hit the heated wok for their initial firing in the factory.

If there is any trauma to the leaf, it certainly doesn't translate to us. It doesn't seem to cross over.

I have always felt that a bit of tea's soul is locked up in the leaf and freed upon infusion. When tea's soul is liberated by the hot water, it seems like the first thing the leaves do is orient themselves to their new surroundings. They balance out, ground, and try to get home. To assist them, I always pour a little of my tea onto the ground before I drink. It is a gesture of thanksgiving, returning to the earth a little of the bounty she so freely gives to us. I also place the spent leaves on bare ground.

Tea seeks to be rooted through us and thus assists us to ground. It is a natural desire of all plants, whose home is in the earth, to want to bring us there. Many people exclaim about their grounding and centering experiences with some teas.

I stay close to the leaves as they steep. I reassure them they are safe to awaken. I sing over them and call to them as they open and yield. As I said before, spiritualizing tea changes its leaf chemistry. Praying over the leaves changes the water as well. I place my hands over the brewing leaves, focus my energy and attention on the tea, and the chi flows out of my palms into my vessel. This ritual raises the vibration of the brew and produces a better-tasting cup, as the experiments of scientist Masaru Emoto have shown.

It may take several attempts, starting over again with fresh leaves, before you bring a tea to its fullest potential. It takes patient experimentation with water temperatures and infusion times before a tea is "fully realized" or as Kakuzo Okakura says, before you can bring out its "noblest expression." Remember, says James Norwood Pratt, what we're trying to do here is "to extract the nectar from the leaf, not cook the nectar." An over-brewed tea will taste dry, bitter, and top heavy; an under-brewed tea, thin and faceless.

And then there are those days when you make a mistake, use the wrong water, over-brew it at the wrong temperature, and the tea tastes great. Some teas are more forgiving than others.

You cannot observe brewing leaves in a teapot, and in a porcelain gaiwan one may only look down on the top of the leaves. When I do use a porcelain gaiwan, I always leave the lid off so I can see what's going on. Most of the time I brew tea in clear glass Pyrex tumblers, though glass gaiwans are now available. It affords me a view from every angle so that I can join the leaves and participate in the entire infusion process. I never cover the glass, in order to provide an opportunity for the union of the tea with the spirit world.

The tumblers I use are fourteen-ounce French jam jars, which equal about two English teacups. The size of these containers enables me to sit for long periods of time undisturbed and undistracted. They're not very aesthetic compared to porcelain gaiwans, but you have to remember that when you are served Dragon Well tea in its home city of Hangzhou, it's always brought to you in a clear glass tumbler. A lot of local folk there, including employees at the Tea Museum and the Tea Research Institute, drink straight out of mason jars.

The glass also permits me to view clouds of downy white hairs that fall from the leaves as they brew. However, for the longest time, the reason I used tumblers was to watch for the occasional face of a soul that had come to take the waters. I would hold the glass up to the sky and peer up through the bottom of the tea watching for a pair of lips to come to kiss the surface of my tea.

And yes, different brewing vessels make the tea taste different, like wine decanted into differently shaped goblets. Personally, I prefer tea brewed in vessels devoid of sharp corners.

I've always been fascinated by the film of tiny bubbles that form on the surface of my tea as the leaves continue to brew. Oftentimes, the fine bubbles look like the swirling clouds depicted in Chinese silks and porcelains. I wonder if this is where they got the image. I think fortunes would be better read from the images discerned within these foaming bubbles than from the spent leaves at the bottom of my cup.

Another fascinating phenomenon I observe appears to be steam caught beneath the surface tension of the water trying to escape and at the same time evaporating immediately when it does escape. The patterns created on the surface of the tea are quite marvelous to behold. They shift about swiftly in odd jerky movements, resembling, at times, a melting ice pack with lots of fissures. If you blow on it the whole thing disappears then slowly returns. Perhaps the patterns are those the steam makes at the point of evaporation, when it separates from the hot water.

The other day I was holding my hands over some brewing leaves watching the steam swirl up into my face. A long, thin column of steam came right up into my eyes and I could actually peer down the funnel onto the clear surface of my tea.

Different leaves exhibit unique qualities with the addition of hot water. Some cluster at the top of the brewing vessel first and then expand and spread out across the surface of the water creating, eventually, a veritable bog of leaves. At a certain point they may all begin to drop to the bottom of the glass. I love the slow leisurely pace with which they fall.

Sometimes when they're all at the top you can see the dark amber colors of the tea begin to drop down and move like clouds through the water. At other times, when the leaves are at the bottom, the colors lie low, staying close to the leaves, until they're stirred up.

As an evergreen, tea leaves grow very slowly compared with deciduous vegetation. Over the years I've learned to brew them slowly as well. I'm not in any race. Brewing tea takes time. Its quiet, subdued nature is part of its allure.

Everything about tea tempers our pace. Cool temperatures at night in the tea fields slow the growth of the leaves, producing a more flavorful cup. Slow brewing with cooler water brings out tea's more noble qualities. The very nature of tea slows us down and makes us appreciate simpler things—a simple stove to place the kettle on, a wooden countertop for the porcelain, soft lighting, peace. I am reminded of the quote by Robert Brault: "Enjoy the little things in life, for one day you may look back and realize they were the big things."

INCANT WHILE YOU DECANT

It is now time to extract the leaves from the water. Your timer may have just gone off or you may simply have intuited that the leaves are ready. The leaves will let you know.

Decant into another container and find a place to sit down for a while.

Though we have pulled the leaves out, there is often residual, particulate leaf matter still brewing in our cups. This is why a tea can taste different with each sip of the first infusion. With certain teas, like some Puerhs, I prefer to let the tea "rest" a full ten minutes after I've withdrawn the leaves, letting it cool to a few degrees above body temperature. In this way a tea may "come to completion," peaking out at full potential.

TASTING

We already have an intimate relationship with this tea, but when our lips break the surface tension of our brew our whole body fills with its essence. We breathe life into the leaves with fire, water, and prayer, and she breathes life into us. We let tea infuse in the cup and then we let the tea infuse in us. Our bodies are now the vessel.

Like the trigram *tui*, the lake or the vessel, in the *I Ching*, only by virtue of its emptiness, its receptivity, can it receive any water at all. It is the same with a lot of spiritual practices. We "empty ourselves" first to become a "receptive vessel" for the guidance and counsel we seek. And so it is with tea. As we sit drinking our tea, savoring its taste, the calm, reflective surface of the lake causes us to reflect, slow down, and withdraw from the world into ourselves to receive what we need.

Cultivating our palates is prerequisite to appreciating tea, but tea is not an experience of the palate alone.

When I am with these young ladies of China, the green and white teas, my faculty of speech is arrested, a hush comes over my body, and if I am standing, I am gently ushered to a chair. When I do manage to offer up a word that describes my experience, the word ethereal comes up. It can be very challenging to try to describe the taste of a tea that is at once haunting, elusive, intangible, and otherworldly.

Tea is of such exquisite delicacy that it resonates with our most fragile sensibilities.

YIXING TEA POTS

Initially, I was not impressed with the pot. It was plain and unattractive. Although I'd never seen an earthenware pot you could boil water in, it was the simple, almost crude, unglazed, micaceous earth I found unappealing. It wasn't even well balanced.

I kept passing by it on the stove of the house where I was working that day. It looked so out of place sitting there on the huge modern six-burner stove, but something about it began to haunt me. It was of such humble stock, its countenance so unimposing, it suggested it didn't want to be noticed at all. It exuded a kind of shyness.

It also began to look familiar. I realized it reminded me of those ancient unassuming pots that grace the first pages of pictorial overviews of Yixing pottery, the kind I tend to skip over to get to newer, more clever pieces. It had the same plain lines and simple beauty that I'd also seen in utilitarian ware from other civilizations.

I finally inquired about it. I learned that it was made of local clay, by a local artisan.

Later I thought, why not brew tea in a vessel crafted from the same soil in which tea bushes sink their roots? And why not use water from springs that rise through that same soil?

If you search for a place like this in China, you will come to Yixing. You will also find in a town nearby the residence of China's most beloved Tea Master, Lu Yu. Perhaps it was the teapot as well as the tea that drew him there.

Although there are no Yixing tea *kettles*, there are thousands of Yixing tea pots, and there is only one place in the world where this very unique purple sand, or Zisha, clay deposits are found. That is in and around this city of Yixing, Jiangsu Province, China.

Yixing, on the shores of Lake Tai (*Tai Hu*), is the capital of China's pottery industry. The first thing that struck me when I entered this town was the smoke from all of the kilns. Ceramics studios and factories crowd both sides of the street.

People often remark upon the small size of Yixing pots when they see them. A typical pot for Chinese tea rituals holds only four ounces of water (English tea cups hold six). For English-style tea drinkers who are used to Brown Bettys or Chatsford pots, even for Japanese tea enthusiasts who brew in those beautiful cast iron pots, this is quite a transition to make, but it is often a very charming one. When you have an opportunity to hold one of these little creations in the palm of your hand, the second thing you notice is their incredible artistry. Each is handmade with the chop mark of the artist on both the bottom of the pot and the underside of the lid. (Be forewarned, however; like everything else, there are cheap, mass-produced imitations.)

There is an entire museum in Yixing dedicated to these pots just as there are massive volumes of pictorial retrospectives. Some cleverly crafted pots, inspired by themes from nature, look like melons or ancient tree trunks, and they fetch thousands of dollars.

The simple lines and unglazed appeal of the more traditional pots used in Chinese tea ceremonies attract tea connoisseurs for two other reasons as well. The first is that the pots are incredibly durable and can withstand radical temperature fluctuations. They don't shatter as easily as porcelain. The second draw for connoisseurs is the porosity of the clay, and this is what you hear most about. In fact, one of my teachers went on so about how porous the clay was that I asked, "Then why don't they leak?"

He couldn't answer at the time, but later I found that the outsides of the pots are constantly tapped with wooden mallets throughout the assembly process. They are also burnished, worked with tools made from buffalo horns. Both techniques compress the clay and seal the pores so that the pot does not leak.

It is only the inside of these pots that contain these thousands and thousands of microscopic air pockets. The clay, in fact, is so porous that it is recommended you only use one very specific type of tea for each pot because the tea infuses the pot, if you will, and renders it useless for other types of tea brewing. It is even recommended that you cure a pot before you use it with the tea you intend to set that pot aside for. This involves simply boiling the pot in a saucepan full of water with the tea that you will use so that the pot becomes saturated with the tea.

Connoisseurs always say that only one tea should be brewed in a Yixing pot for its entire life, but this is not necessarily so. Tastes change over the years, and if you find you want to use a "cured and seasoned pot" for a different tea, all you need do is refire it. This will clean or "sterilize" it so that you can begin again. Unfortunately, it may compromise the pot's valued patina which the collectors prize.

There are devotees that swear by the enhanced taste of tea brewed in these pots, and it is easy to see how this would be so. First, it has no corners or sharp edges that would upset the chi of the brewing process. Second, a seasoned pot will impart unique flavors to the brew from past use. Third, when brewing tea in a traditional manner, the tiny pots are often placed in a "tea boat" or Yixing tea bowl. This is so that boiling hot water may be poured upon the top of the pot to keep it hot. This also changes the convection currents within the pot as the leaves brew and, for some, enhances the taste.

TEA WITH MARJORIE SEGELL

One day while working at a private home, my client said to me, "Oh, Frank, I saw some tea at the grocery store the other day

I thought you might like so I bought it. Let's have some!"

I couldn't have been more pleased. Nobody ever makes me tea! "Well, that's a wonderful idea, Marjorie. Yes, let's take a break!"

She filled her kettle with tap water and placed it on the stove. She then reached up into a cabinet in her kitchen and pulled down a plain white porcelain teapot and into the infuser basket of that pot she placed three Stash Earl Grey teabags. While we waited for the water to boil she set the table with two place settings, a bowl of sugar, and another bowl topped off with Coffee Mate.

When the tea was ready, I did the honors and poured us both a mug of the stuff. And to my cup I added a heaping teaspoon of Coffee Mate and a half teaspoon of sugar. It tasted so good I filled my mug twice more, and we had a grand old time.

Marjorie Segell is an elderly English woman who'd just spent ten weeks in the hospital. She had lost a son many years ago and recently a husband. I had just lost a daughter and, years ago, a wife. I was so moved that Marjorie had thought of me enough to buy what for her was a special brand, and that she just went ahead and made it without any fuss. Mostly, though, I was touched by her sincerity.

These are the moments of graciousness we all experience when it comes to tea etiquette. Moments of humility when someone makes a genuine effort to reach out to us. When human needs require greater attendance, tea's role is secondary.

Understand, if tea is going to speak to you, if tea is going to enter your heart and change your life, it will do so no matter how it is packaged, processed, or presented, no matter where it is from, how old it is, or how it is brewed. Whether a rare and priceless tea from a remote and exotic tea garden in China or your basic brand X, it doesn't matter. Whether in a Yixing pot or a Mason jar, if your intentions are honorable and you approach tea with reverence and respect, there is no wrong way to make it.

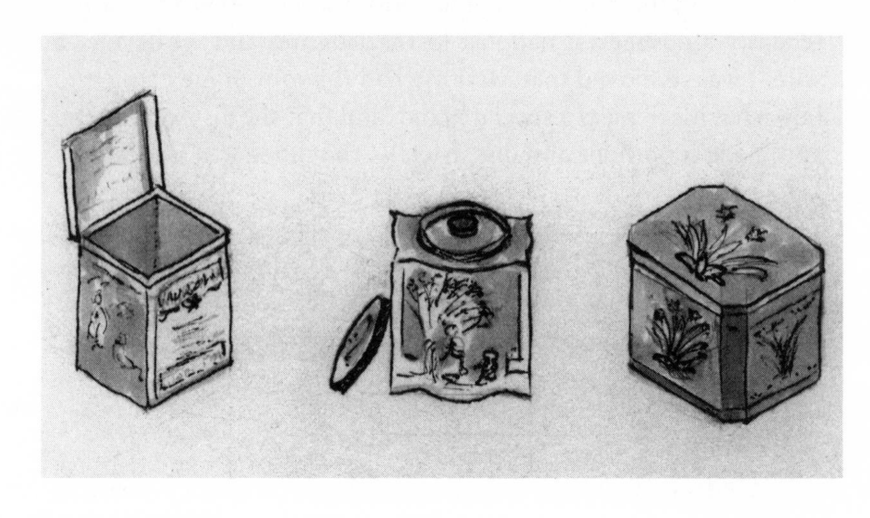

IV

THE CAST OF CHARACTERS

TEAS ARE SO UNIQUE in appearance and flavor that the Chinese created six different categories to describe them. The classical groupings look like this:

White teas
Yellow teas
Green teas
Oolong teas
Black teas (or Red in China)
Puerh teas

Although some white teas can be rich and full bodied and some blacks can be quite delicate, as you drop through the list, the teas become more and more manipulated, the stages of their production get longer and more complicated, and the tastes generally get stronger and bolder. The white, yellow, and green teas are subtle and more delicate in flavor, and they are processed the least. The oolongs, blacks, and Puerhs are deep, rich, and full-bodied. As you pass down through the list, the caffeine content increases, too.

What distinguishes each tea from the other in these six categories is the amount of time that lapses between the moment the leaves are picked and the moment those leaves are exposed to high heat. Once they are exposed to heat, the oxidation process is arrested and the breakdown of the leaves' enzymes ceases. A green tea, for example, may be brewed the same day it is picked. The leaves are harvested, laid out to dry or wither for a short period of time, and then exposed to high heat in an open wok. The oolongs and blacks are often roughed up a bit, crushed, battered, and bruised to accelerate the enzyme breakdown and create the tastes that distinguish them as oolongs or blacks. Often they are fired several times. Each tea is processed in a unique style, and on top of that, every farm does it a little differently.

Beyond the processing, certain tea bushes lend themselves better to certain types of tea. For example, the iron-rich soil and subtropical climate in Fujian province produce large-leaf white and oolong teas. In contrast, the four seasons of Zhejiang province are best suited for the smaller leaves of green teas.

These factors all contribute, along with their internal yin and yang, to the distinctive character of individual teas.

THRESHOLD TEAS

I would like to introduce you to six special teas, one from each category. I call them threshold teas. A threshold is a place of entrance, a doorway into a part of ourselves or into the tea plant itself, where information may be accessed that is not normally available to us. This "information" may come in the form of intuitive insights, premonitions, and inspirational thoughts. It may also make our feelings run the gamut from wonderful to uneasy. Threshold teas have changed my experience and understanding of the plant, the universe, and myself—teas that have taken me on journeys, invited me into altered spaces, shared with me their stories and songs.

There are some teas that are capable of taking us to some rather extraordinary places and because of this are initiatory rites unto themselves. While you may have to go outside of yourself to procure your tea, in the end, it is the tea that brings you home.

If tea becomes a daily devotional practice and you approach it with an open heart and an open mind, the five Taoist elements balance themselves, the information you seek presents itself, and there will be no wrong tea and no wrong way to make it.

Yinzhen, or Silver Needle

In my cup
Yinzhen buds drop their down
Like a light spring snow,
And in the orchard where I sit
Petals fall
Through the flowering branches of the plum.
Even the clouds are descending.
They have left the sky.
They've come to kiss the tea on Junshan mountain.
Or perhaps they've come to carry home
The spirits of the leaves
As they rise in the steam
Rolling off my cup
Seeking to join the mother mist making its way to Yueyang County.

Silver Needle teas are exclusively leaf buds. When they have been steeping for a period of time they become soft and pliable enough to be opened manually. Inside the bud one often finds several undeveloped leaves wrapped tightly around a tiny immature leaf bud at the center. Hairs grow on the underside of the leaf. The buds, when dried, are so heavily laden with downy hairs that they appear white. Thus, Silver Needle teas are characterized as white teas. Also, the cup often yields "white" or clear liquor.

China whites are from Fujian province, across from Taiwan. All the most popular white teas are plucked from the same bush in the tea gardens. At the Tea Museum in Hangzhou, there is an illustration of a tea twig showing the Chinese names of the first three leaves of new growth on the bush. The first leaf bud or tip at the end of the twig is Yinzhen, or Silver Needle. The second leaf (an opened leaf) is called *Gong Mei*, and the third largest and fully opened leaf is called Shou Mei.

There are three types of China white teas: *Yin Zhen* or Silver Needle, composed solely of leaf buds; *Bai Mudan*, *Pai Mutan* or

White Peony, a combination of leaf buds and whole leaves; and *Shou Mei* or Longevity Eyebrows, whole leaves without any buds at all. A lot of White Peony teas are stitched together to form a "rosette" where the leaf buds are tied together at their base and radiate out from a common center to form a circle. When this rosette is infused and swells up, it is reminiscent of a peony flower. The third and final harvesting produces *Shou Mei*, a rather pedestrian tea, comparatively. Many exporting countries now utilize white tea production techniques to create teas like white Darjeeling.

White teas are the least manipulated by man, though most are steamed or exposed to high temperatures somewhere during their processing. Some tea companies may claim their white teas are left out in the open to air dry, but unless the owners themselves are witnesses in the field, it may not be the case. One year, the Imperial Tea Court offered an air-dried white tea, the production of which was overseen by Roy Fong. It tasted unlike any white I'd ever had—full-bodied with hints of honey, toasted wheat, fresh green hay, and light florals.

White teas are purported to contain more healthful benefits than green teas, especially in regard to antioxidant content. I believe, therefore, that the less a tea is manipulated the more potent its curative properties.

Silver Needle teas can be deliciously full-bodied, sweet, and calming. Tea's relaxing agent, L-Theanine, has a greater chance to express itself because white teas contain the least amount of caffeine. There is not much competition going on between tea's stimulating properties and its relaxing agent. As a result, some white teas have transported me into deep trance-like meditative states. In biofeedback terminology, they're called alpha and theta states. I call them "trance teas." Sometimes in the fall, I'll add a few chrysanthemum petals to my Yinzhen. These ghostly white angels appear to attach themselves to each rising bud as if assisting them to the top of the cup.

> I sat on the side of the hill. Above me giant ponderosas towered. The entire canyon was filled with them. Each needle of the pines sparkled and glistened in the high desert sun. I was mes-

merized by each silver needle, as the branches moved in the breeze. And in my glass, I watched how the silver needles of my tea sparkled and glistened in the sun, moving in the currents of their downy wake as if in the breezes of the canyon.

When most people think of tea strength, they think of a dark color, a strong taste, or a high-caffeine content, but I have found that white teas, though subtle in color, taste, and caffeine, contain powerful centering and grounding agents. It may not always be the taste of a tea that keeps me coming around to it but its effects on my temperament and psyche.

Frequently when drinking Yinzhen, I have the sensation of my energy and attention being pulled into myself at a point at the back of my throat. It is an astringent action, if you will, not of dryness but of gathering.

Junshan Yinzhen

MY INITIAL EXPERIENCE OF JUNSHAN YINZHEN

First sip: The world evaporates as I re-enter my crown chakra, gathering my energy back into myself.

Second sip: All tension in my head and shoulders dissipates and I drop into the fourth chakra where this tea soothes my heart.

Third sip: Energy continues to drop into my belly as I sink deeper into myself.

Fourth sip: Tension in my body continues to subside and I drop to my pelvic floor in an alpha state.

Fifth sip: State of being after an hour of bodywork. My vertebrae realign voluntarily.

Sixth sip: At one with myself. I was able to read the fine print on medicine bottles without my reading glasses.

Seventh sip: At one with the autumn soil, the earth.

Eighth sip: All things are at hand as my pelvis yields to the wisdom body.

Ninth sip: My soul is awash in this calming evergreen leaf. There is time for everything.

Tenth sip: I'm home! There is nothing left to achieve.

Junshan Yinzhen, from Yueyang county in Hunan province, is a yellow tea that is said to have been a personal favorite of Chairman Mao's. Yellow teas have an extra step added to their production that makes them different from other teas. The extra step is called "sealed yellowing," where either bamboo mats are laid down on top of the withering leaves for anywhere from three hours to several days, or the leaves are wrapped in paper. This turns the leaves slightly yellow and imparts unique flavor.

Junshan Yinzhen has a smoky taste that makes you wonder if, when it was fired, smoke from the coals beneath the woks suffused the leaves. Initially, I did not identify this flavor as smoke, as a lot of people do. To me, it had a different quality. It turns out it is the natural taste of the leaves. Because of its distinctive taste, it is often served in Hunan with strong-tasting foods.

With a name like Yinzhen, I assumed the Junshan Yinzhen was a white tea, but the term yinzhen, or silver needle, refers to an identifiable leaf style—a white or silvery needle-shaped leaf bud. Other leaf style names are *mao feng* (flat and pointy with hair), *mao jian* (round and pointy with hair), *hao cha* (hairy or downy tea), bai hao (white hairs), *hao ya* (small bud), *yin hao* (silver down), *zhu cha* (pearl shaped tea leaves) and *huang ya* (yellow bud). These leaf styles describe the shape of the leaf once the tea is finished, for instance, whether the leaves are wiry and twisted as in a *mao feng*, rolled into a ball as in the various gunpowder teas, or flattened as a Dragon Well would be.

The buds of these "tippy" Silver Needle teas are often so tight that a hotter water temperature is recommended. When I received my first 2.5-gram box of Junshan Yinzhen from the Imperial Tea Court, I brewed it like a green tea. When Grace Fong made it for me with near-to-boiling water, it was a completely different tea.

Dragon Well, or Lung Ching

One does not often equate the soul with material possessions, but when I had my first taste of Dragon Well, it was as if my soul had just slipped on a hand embroidered silk waistcoat.

Once when I held my tea aloft in an offertory gesture, I thought I saw a face come to sip my Dragon Well. Its features were cast in the steam rolling off my cup. It startled me so my heart retracted and the face withdrew.

It is not an empty gesture I make when I offer my first cup. I invoke individuals from the spirit world to join me, and if one is called upon to attend, why should it frighten me so?

When you invoke their names often enough, they will come.

Dragon Well is China's most popular and well-known green tea. As Roy Fong reminds us, it is famous for its "four uniques": jade color in the cup, vegetative aroma in the nose, mellow chestnut flavor in the mouth, and singular appearance to the eye—flat, straight leaves pointed at the tip and of uniform size.

Dragon Well is grown on various estates in the West Lake district of Hangzhou, Zhejiang province, which is approximately sea level. Sometimes I refer to Hangzhou as China's "Tea Central" because it is there we find China's National Tea Museum and The Tea Research Institute, known for its annual green tea competition. It was Dragon Well tea that early Japanese monks became so enamored of when they came to study Chan Buddhism at a nearby monastery. I believe the taste of Dragon Well inspired the creation of their own Sencha teas when they returned to Japan. Tea has been grown in monastic settings for thousands of years to foster meditative practices, both as a stimulant and a relaxant. It also allays hunger and other appetites.

Dragon Well gets its unique flat shape and glossy sheen during the initial firing process in the wok. Once the wok is fired up to a temperature of approximately 120–140 degrees Celsius, tea oil is applied to the metal surface of the wok and the leaves are thrown in. The leaves are pressed down by the hand on the bottom of the wok, and in circular movements slid up upon the sides of the wok and flipped back to the bottom again, where the process starts over. Pushing down on the leaves makes them flat. Sliding them up the side of the wok polishes them.

The Dragon Well harvest begins in late March. Some years, if there is a late frost or heavy rain, there may be no Dragon Well at all! This is a travesty for the connoisseur because the harvest is one of the most anticipated events of the entire year. The leaves are bright green and there's an effervescence to the brew. Of course, there is nothing like having a tea the same day it was picked and brewed with local spring water in its own native hills. One of the crowning experiences of any Chinese Tea Tour is to pick your own Dragon Well tea, fire it yourself, and then hike up to Tiger Run Spring to collect the water to brew it with. Water from this spring has an extremely high surface tension that actually keeps coins afloat. Pouring it slowly out of a glass, it hangs over the edge before the tension breaks, like liquid mercury. There are some experiences that forever changed my relationship with tea and this is one of them.

Green teas are forever being advertised as unoxidized, or what used to be referred to erroneously as "unfermented." If you watch how they are harvested and processed you will see that is not the case. *All* teas are oxidized to some degree. The instant a leaf is separated from the bush it begins to break down, to oxidize. It may take an hour or two or even the next day for some tea leaves to hit that heated wok.

Green teas always seem to hold up under multiple infusions better than any other tea. You'd think it would be the other way around. You'd think a deep, rich black tea would have more sustaining power, but this is not what I've observed. I've never made four, five, or six infusions from any tea other than a green. It may be that the life force and thus the chemistry of fresh new green leaves are so concentrated that this tea supports multiple infusions.

A friend once described the taste of each consecutive cup like a bird slowly flying away. Another friend suggested that re-steeping the leaves brought out, what he called, the more adult flavors. Some may describe the taste as weaker with each cup. I just call it different.

Da Hong Pao, or The Big Red Robe

Once I saw
The deep ambers of my oolong
Jump and dance
As the sun streamed through my glass
And cast its golden shadows
At my feet.

Da Hong Pao is a Fujian Wu Yi Yan Cha Oolong. The Wu Yi Tea District is unique because it is a valley encircled by fifty-six mountain peaks creating its own microclimate. *Yan Chas* are translated variously as "rock" or "cliff"' teas because of the rugged terrain that comprises this unusual sixty-square-kilometer area. The famous four bushes of Da Hong Pao grow on the side of a rock wall at the head of Nine Dragons Stream Canyon. It is an extraordinary hike up to the pagoda where the bushes grow. You may rest and have tea there made with the water from the stream. The day I was there, our tea mistress had stuffed the gaiwan so full of tea that the leaves rose a full inch above the cup after the third infusion. It was how we all felt, overflowing with the generosity of the place, the joy, the stillness, the beauty. The holy Tao moved through the canyon and through the waters of Nine Dragons Stream.

As you wander up the canyon, you begin to notice that there are two different kinds of tea bushes growing there: the smaller-leafed Da Hong Pao that has been coaxed down the canyon, and the larger-leafed and equally famous *Shui Xian*. I have heard Shui Xian translated as Water Sprite, Narcissus, even Praying to the Immortals.

The legends of how this tea got its name vary, but the theme is the same. A government official was in the area when he took ill. He was nursed back to health with the local tea. When he recovered, he sought out the bushes from which the tea was made, lit incense before them, and placed his imperial red cloak over them as an offering.

Once I made this tea for a friend who didn't care for the first infusion. When I presented her with the second infusion she said, "Ah! I see it has exchanged its peasant's cloak for a monk's robe!" Some even claim that the more refined aspects of Da Hong Pao reveal themselves in the third infusion, when the tea drops its monk's robe to don a bishop's vestments.

Oolong teas present a vast array of tasting experiences because they have the widest oxidation range. Green oolongs are closer to green teas; while black, red, or dark oolongs are closer to black teas. And then of course, there is everything in between. The Bao Zhong or Pouchong teas are a subclass within the oolong family and represent a group of teas that are oxidized the least.

To say that oolongs are simply semi-oxidized doesn't do them justice. Some are lightly oxidized, some heavily. It is not my intention to discuss tea production methods; I leave that to others. Suffice it to say, the production of oolongs is complex—a process of picking, withering, indoor oxidation and shaking, tumble heating, rolling, stir frying, kneading, and drying.

The word *oolong*—or *wu-long*—means "black dragon." It is my understanding that "black dragon" derives from the black serpentine shape of certain Anxi County Tieguanyins, a leaf shape one sees at competitions, although there are many teas whose "twist" looks dragon like. In the high misty crags of these mountains you would expect to see a dragon or two.

Dian Hong

Even when the water's quiet
And the buds are still
Downy white hairs will rise
In mysterious mythical mudras
In the unseen currents of my cup.

Most tea companies offer a Dian Hong of one grade or another, usually under the name of Yunnan Gold. Like Puerh, it is a large-leafed variety. There are often flavor notes in Yunnan Golds reminiscent of a Puerh, but Dian Hongs have their own signature tastes and hold their own. After it is brewed, Dianhong's leave a dark amber film on the inside of a white gaiwan, so thick and syrupy is the liquor. The leaves contain so much down that thick concentrations of fine white hair still linger on the bottom of a glass after the third infusion.

This is the tea I often refer to as my "soul retrieval tea" because of its ability to resuscitate me from the depths. It is the only tea that can bring me back from the edge. If I am immobilized by lethargy or emotionally stranded by a black mood, this is the tea that "jump starts my chi" or more graciously, gently wakens my inner furnaces. Besides that, I love the taste! Peppery, malty, deep, complex, rich!

I once had an experience with a Dian Hong called Jinhuang Dianhong Cha. It was the grand champion of a 1995 competition. Jinhuang is the name of the town where the tea is harvested and in Chinese, Dian Hong simply means Yunnan Red. The Tea Masters Association that sponsored the competition was so impressed with the tea that they bought the entire harvest. I had tasted it at the competition and was so impressed that I kept track of its ownership and consistently lobbied to acquire some more of it. Five or six years after the harvest, I finally got a sample of Jinhuang Dian Hong Cha. When I received the tea, it took a while to create the space necessary to brew it in an honorable way. Finally, alone at a friend's house, I brought purified water, my finest porcelain, and all my equipage out to a side portal with sweeping views of the Sangre de Cristo Mountain Range. It was a warm spring day. Gramma grasses swayed in the morning breeze and huge cumulus clouds drifted in from Arizona.

I made a large pot of Jinhuang Dian Hong Cha so I could sit undisturbed for a long time in the tea's presence. Though the tea was old and most of its immediate impact had withered and waned, it still retained some of it finer qualities. These manifested at the back of the palate and made me realize that, yes, there was still some life left in this old friend of mine.

Some folks may have spit it out, claiming it had "gone off," that it was stale and useless. They would not have given it a chance. But I had created a space for the tea to speak, and in the end, Thea finished with her complex notes, offering up her lasting strength and beauty.

I sat there for forty-five minutes until I felt energy shoot out from my hips and drop to the ground. Shortly after that a smaller umbrella of energy shot out sideways, and it, too, fell to the ground, dropping a foot below the surface of the earth. I had merged with the essence of the leaf.

After this, even when the scalding tea splashed over my hand or spilled down my chest, I never dropped the Dian Hong! Her spirit stayed with me for weeks, allowing me to feel strong, grounded, focused. To pay homage to her, I have thought of placing her spent leaves in a silk shroud and burying them in the ground. But today, what seems best is to spread them out in the sun.

I thought of all the love and attention that went into making this tea. How it had been groomed to win competitions. How it was the end of a perfect tea year. How everything had come together flawlessly: the climate and rainfall, the soil and elevation, the moment of picking and processing. All the right conditions, too, when I brewed the tea: the right water and water temperature, the right amount of leaf, and the length of infusion time. And lastly, my choice of timing: a moment when I was particularly quiet, receptive, and available.

Kakuzo Okakura writes, "Tea is a work of art and needs a master hand to bring out its noblest qualities.... Each preparation of the leaves has its individuality, its special affinity with water and heat, its hereditary memories to recall, its own method of telling a story." Okakura's reflections align with the current theory of the maverick English scientist Rupert Sheldrake, who describes "morphic resonance fields" as a place where we may actually be able to tap into a plant's memory or the memory of the whole species.

PUERH

In ancient Taoist texts one is often forewarned about practicing certain techniques without the guidance of a qualified teacher. But there are no such forewarnings on tins of certain teas.

While the Cantonese name of this tea from Yunnan province is Pou-Nei, most people are familiar with its Mandarin names, Puerh, Pu-erh, or Puer. It is the tea that has changed my life. There has been more misinformation disseminated about this tea than any other, probably because so little was known about it, and the information I present here may not be absolute.

Over the years, an array of theories has been offered about how Puerh may have come into being. The most accurate account appeared recently in a book called *The Empire of Tea* by Alan and Iris Macfarlane: "There is a custom that survives today among the tribal people of northern Burma in which wild jungle tea leaves are prepared by boiling and kneading. The leaves are then wrapped up in papers or stuffed into 'the internodes of bamboo' that they bury in underground silos for several months to ferment." To this day, some Puerhs are stored and sold in bamboo shafts, which impart a unique flavor to the tea.

After keeping a bowl of spent leaves on my kitchen counter for several days, a mold grows on top of the leaves. I can imagine a tea farmer hard on his luck after several poor seasons dipping into a pile of leaves and unearthing a very unusual-tasting tea. Maybe this is what happened in China.

The Puerh leaf is of the large Dai Yeh variety. Its antecedents trace their lineage back to the mother tea trees of China, the wisdom keepers of the species, as I call them. It is Puerh that is the staple tea of the Manchurians, Mongolians, and Tibetans.

All Puerhs start as green tea. We do not often associate Puerh with the new green teas available first thing in the spring, but such is its extraordinary versatility. There are green Puerhs, black Puerhs, even white, or Silver Needle Puerhs. They can come as a loose-leaf tea or in dense bricks or cakes in all shapes and sizes. It may be enjoyed as a fresh green tea the day it is picked or it may be permitted to age for many years. It is one of the very few teas, as with some oolongs, that improves with age. The trick is to invest in a Puerh you know will age well; that only comes with experience. Connoisseurs will buy quantities of their favorite grade to store in a cool, dry, place away from light. Unlike other teas, you do not need to keep Puerhs in airtight containers. They thrive best loosely wrapped or where there's some minimal movement of air.

Some may dispute the fact that a Puerh may be enjoyed the day it is harvested. They might say that, technically, it is not a Puerh at all because it is not fermented. I submit that we should open the classification to include all teas made with the Puerh leaf, no matter how they are processed.

At first, I did not like the taste of green Puerhs. I thought them rough, raw, and coarse, but once I started dipping into some aged white, Silver Needle Puerh cakes, I began to cultivate a taste for the greens. My preference, though, is for the blacks. Listen to a description by Roy Fong of one of his own black Puerhs: "Presents a sweet sugar cane nose with a cacao bean undertone. Enters smooth on the tongue and releases a complex mouthful of flavors reminiscent of a Black Yunnan. The bright red cup presents a gold rim on the edge, which is a distinctive sign of quality. Finishes with complex aftertastes of a freshly rolled Havana cigar. Wood, air, metal, water and earth—the five elements—are all in balance with this wonderful tea. A rapture of the senses! Very far from the cliché of moldy low-grade Puerh products."

All Puerhs are undeniably an acquired taste. People are amazed to see how dark the liquor is when I serve them a cup. It often brews up as black as coffee. Some recoil from its appearance, saying, "Oh, that looks too strong for me!" But once they taste it, they find it is not as strong as it looks.

The popular black Puerh variety, which some describe as a dark green Puerh, becomes black via the fermentation process. Puerhs are the only teas that are fermented in the proper sense of the word, where there is the actual presence of mold or bacterium. The leaves are permitted to compost with the addition of water, under controlled conditions. It is sometimes fun to experiment with enhancing or changing the taste of a Puerh by roasting the leaves slowly in an oven for a few minutes or by misting the leaves with water and letting them dry completely over a day or two.

It is wise to rinse the leaves with hot water briefly before you brew them. This will "clean" the leaves and cut some of its musty aroma. There are some Puerhs, on the other hand, that I prefer not to rinse.

There are so many air pockets locked up in Puerh that when I do not rinse the tea, the lid of my gaiwan starts popping off the bowl, clinking and clanking as the air escapes. I love Puerh when boiling water is first poured on it. With all the air pockets locked up in it, it starts to bubble and fizz. The leaves are actually experiencing thousands of little orgasms when they are reunited with water. I call this precise moment "the ecstasy of the leaves."

Puerh is purported to have all kinds of healthful properties, from being a digestive to cutting fats in our blood, which lowers cholesterol. Personally, I've noticed no reduction in my cholesterol levels. What I have noticed is that it beneficially changes the flora in my intestinal tract, especially if I've contracted an intestinal bug or flu. While it is recommended to rinse Puerh lightly before you brew it, any rinsing will lessen the bacterial potency helpful in warding off the grippe.

Puerh is also said to be good for hangovers. I can personally attest to its efficacy in that regard.

Puerh is not a laxative but it is a gentle digestive. Sometimes, the very thought of making myself a cup of Puerh stimulates my entire alimentary system. It not only helps our bodies to dissolve the fats we take in during a meal, it also acts like digestive enzymes to digest that meal. The bacterium in the tea acts as a tonic upon the intestinal tract, stimulating digestion and elimination. You may notice you are a little bit more "regular" than normal and find yourself using the bathroom at an unusual hour.

When I lecture about tea, the audience is often curious about a possible connection between Puerh tea and the Latin word *puer*, adapted by Carl Gustav Jung in his analysis of *puer aeternus*, or "eternal boy." There is no connection. I am actually much more intrigued by making the association of Puerh tea with a particular female Taoist Immortal, Sun Puerh, that figures prominently in Eva Wong's book *Seven Taoist Masters*. Ms. Wong writes that Puerh here translates as "no second way." Interestingly, there is a brand of Puerh called Nor Sun Puerh!

100 Winning Teas

National Tea Competition, Hangzhou, China
Sponsored by the Chinese Academy of Agricultural Sciences Tea Research Institute

Were it not for the concerted efforts of Roy and Grace Fong and Donald Wallis, these translations would not exist. Some of these names describe the taste of the tea in our mouth; others describe the experience of the tea in our body. Listening to these names, we are reminded of the close connection between tea and poetry in Chinese culture.

1. Celestial Lake of Jade Bamboo
2. Royal Autumn Cloud
3. Evening Snow Diamonds
4. Poem of the Silver Lantern
5. Reflection of the Phoenix
6. Dragon Brook
7. Star Shadows on Celestial Lake of Jade Bamboo
8. Secret of the Weeping Willow
9. Scampering Ermin
10. Seclusion of the Silver Parasol
11. Sigh of the Sapphire
12. Phantom Palm
13. Imperial Cloudmist
14. The Sorcerer's Plum
15. Great Sword of the Dragon
16. Eclipse of Spring Romance
17. Blushing Lotus
18. Fragrant Glow of Spring
19. The Valiant Canary
20. The Treasure of the Valiant Canary Mountain
21. Lingering Emerald Cascade
22. Lonely Artist
23. Eternal Dragon
24. Jade Snowflake
25. Moonbean Silhouette on Silver Mountain
26. Thousand Dragon
27. Song of the Ivory Butterfly
28. Shrine of the Pale Green Tortoise
29. The Emperor's Magic Signet
30. Morning Mist on Golden Mountain
31. Echoes of Respendent Mandarins
32. Call of the Green Gull
33. Tong Ling Bird's Tongue
34. Gallant Mask of Mirth
35. Sleeping Silver Elephant
36. Golden Eye of the Phoenix
37. Ba Shan Bird's Tongue
38. Imperial Jade Ring
39. Down of the Damask Glove

40. Floating Flower
41. Spring Interlude
42. Falling Brooks Soft Duet
43. Curious Drifting Cloud
44. Lair of the Green Dragon
45. Bamboo of Paradise
46. Emerald Nocturne
47. Wistful Glen of Pewter Fog
48. The Ambassador's Jeweled Sash
49. Verdant Velvet Prelude
50. Wisp of the Whisker
51. Dare of the Pink Dagger
52. Bi Luo Chun
53. Portal of the Elder Swallow
54. The Silent Snow Swan
55. Pebble Beach
56. Muse of the Chartreuse Slipper
57. Dancing Snow Petals
58. Satin Breeze
59. Temptation of the Sable Tassle
60. Pirouette of the Dancing Cloud
61. Silence of the Silver Saber
62. Crowing Cock at Dawn
63. Bell of the Immortals
64. Jade Sunset
65. Silver Lace
66. Spring Fortune
67. Winter Wreath of Silver Down
68. Rising Golden Fog
69. Jade Dream
70. Travertine Twilight on Venerable Mountain
71. The Prophesy of Rocky Canyon
72. Frosty Needle Pine Bough
73. Thousand Mountain
74. Silver Tapestry
75. Spring Dragon
76. Mysterious Moon Bouquet
77. Eloquent Embrace
78. Quaint Village
79. Gliding Cloud on Radiant Sunbeam
80. Queen of Tibet
81. Jade View
82. Hundred Fruit
83. The Emerald Lance
84. Snow Dragon
85. Mirage of the Tranquil Tiger
86. Enchanted Snow Blossom
87. Gold Castle Green Cloud
88. Happy Golden Monkey
89. Pearl of the Phoenix
90. Rain Flower
91. Shy Panda
92. The Jade Cavalier
93. Shimmering Canopy of Spring
94. Rising Jade Star
95. Lazy Water Lily
96. Pillars of Heaven
97. Flying Dragon
98. Promise of Silken Sails
99. Ring of the Nine Dragons
100. Emerald Mountain Gold Nectar

YIELD TO THE TEA

All tea requires our utmost attention. They seem to demand a one-on-one relationship with us. It is almost as if we are urged to ask: What is it about this particular tea that makes it taste the way it does? What is it about this tea that makes me feel the way I do? It is my experience with the cast of characters I have introduced here that when drinking tea there is a certain moment of transition that shifts me out of my rational, inquisitive mind into a deeper place, a place of wisdom. As I yield to the tea, descending down into my body, doorways open and I cross over thresholds that once seemed impassable, if not unimaginable.

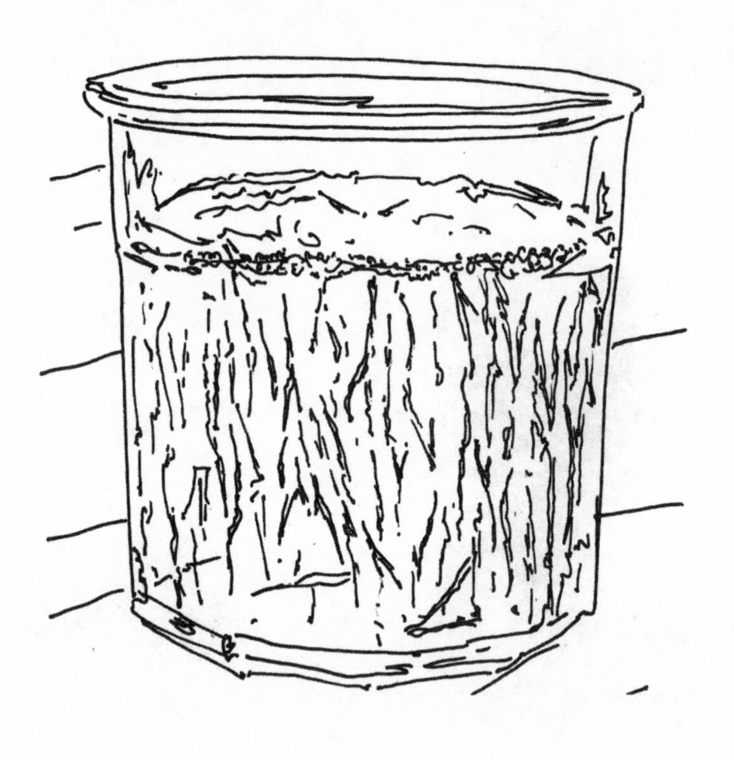

V

DISCERNING TASTE

Heated water fills the pot
And China is liberated.
Ancient minerals
Held in clay
Pass into my bloodstream.

The songs she sings,
Altering synapses,
Turn my body to her dream
And everything her earth had held
Is now holding me.

THE EXPERIENCE OF TEA is a full body experience. A tea worth its weight will carry us deep into a world of refinement that we may not know existed.

Sometimes it is hard to tell whether we are tasting something or smelling it. Our taste buds are really limited to only four sensations: sweetness, sourness, saltiness, and bitterness. Combinations of these four create flavor. We can also feel the viscosity of a fluid—its texture, temperature, and smoothness.

"The palate" was always a vague term to me until I looked it up. It seems to have two definitions. I was familiar with the general description as in someone having a refined palate, but its anatomy eluded me. The palate, I've discovered, is the roof of the mouth consisting of a bony, hard palate in the front and a fleshly, soft palate in the back. The only part of the actual palate that has any taste buds is the soft palate in the back. So there is the physical palate in our mouth, and a generalized term for the whole sense of taste—*all* the organs involved in the sense of taste.

The majority of our taste buds are on our tongue, but they are also on the soft palate; the pharynx, the opening at the back of the mouth; and the epiglottis, the leaf-shaped flap behind the root of the tongue that covers our wind pipe when we swallow.

It is pure genetics as to how many taste buds per square inch we have. In his book *All About Tea*, William Ukers reminds us that tea tasters are born not made.

The olfactory nerve, our sense of smell, is just as involved as the taste buds in discerning the essence of tea. The olfactory nerve is the only part of the human brain that is exposed to open air. The nerve itself sits on, and actually passes through, a bone called the cribriform plate, which is a very porous structure. In fact, the Latin root of cribriform, *cribum*, means "sieve-like." The cribriform plate is part of the ethmoid bone in our sinus, or nasal cavity. The olfactory nerve is also unique in that a portion of it is attached to one of the oldest parts of the brain, the amygdala, an anatomical structure we share with reptiles. It is said that our sense of smell is the most primitive sense we have. It is certainly more sophisticated than our taste buds because not only can it distinguish between complex fragrances, it also has the capability to sense danger in the air, like the smell of a predatory animal.

Another interesting fact: While all the other senses are routed through the thalamus, only the sense of smell is not. It is a self-contained unit that appears to have developed separately from the other senses.

To track a tea in our bodies and discern the complexities of its influence require that we call upon all our faculties, not just our senses. James Norwood Pratt writes: "We may not always be in a condition to register the subtle effects tea has upon us." True, but I say, why not help create the conditions, the consciousness, that would empower us to experience those subtleties.

I rarely have tea in the morning because my palate never seems to be awake at that time. I cannot taste all of tea's most subtle characteristics until I've been up for a while and my palate has had a chance to awaken as well. I've noticed that when I have tea in the morning and again later, the taste of that afternoon tea is always disappointing. The later I wait to have tea, the better it tastes. Morning tea also throws off my "body timing" for the whole day. It's just my own constitution.

My practice is not to eat any food for at least an hour before I have tea to help sensitize my palate. After a while I began to realize that refined teas refine me—and my palate. I have had teas whose fragrance changed with every breath and whose taste changed with every sip. That is why it is important not to judge a tea by the first sip. Hang out with it for a while. Let it affect you. The same tea can taste different at different times of the day. As the sun shifts through the heavens, so do our physiology, our mood, and our mouth chemistry.

It is easy to lose oneself in the depths of taste sensations one encounters in the leaf, with its broad range of expressions. Its song, its story, changes with each infusion. Sometimes it seems that the taste of the first infusion is dominated by the delicate downy white hairs; the second, by the leaf itself; and the third, by the leaf's central, woody vein. Drinking a lot of tea at one sitting may ultimately overwhelm your experience of it or deaden its more subtle qualities and effects.

It is also easy to be seduced by a spectacular-tasting tea and then have the experience go no further than the palate. Darjeeling (Darling-Jing or the "darling" of tea connoisseurs) can be like this. I expect more of a tea than just the taste. If a tea has no depth it cannot sustain a relationship. Darjeelings have depth of taste, yes, but not the depth of engagement of China teas that have always involved me on a deeper, more soulful level where there is an actual dialogue, an exchange. Darjeelings beckon; they make overtures, but to me, it feels like a tease. Maybe in time I will become more receptive.

Darjeeling's charm is seductive
But I have already seen the dancing girls of the marketplace,
Seen the glitter and gleam of the rubied raj
Smelled the grasses crushed beneath my feet at the temple gates
And felt cool breezes blow down from Dharamsala.
Yes, I admit, I was detained,
Like Odysseus at Ogygia,
But after my third cup
I was already paddling
Up the headwaters of the Brahmaputra
Looking for a passage back
Into the thick green hills of Yunnan.

One sip of China tea
And I'm drinking with the immortals.
Heaven fills with a thousand souls.

When I learned that Darjeeling is predominately a China leaf I was surprised. I began to wonder what got lost in translation here. What happened when the English transplanted this bush from China to India? Was the weather so different, the soil, the elevation, the processing? Perhaps so. And why do people continue to classify Darjeeling as a black tea when it looks and tastes like an oolong?

If I'm in the mood for a spectacular-tasting tea that has depth, I'll drink an Oriental Beauty varietal from Taiwan. Here are all the heady, fruity, honey-kissed, deeply satisfying notes I admire in an oolong. Of his own Imperial Bai Hao Formosa Oolong, another name for Oriental Beauty, Roy Fong writes: "It is flamboyantly aromatic, its taste and perfume often reminiscent of ripe peaches, but in any case more deliciously fruity than any other tea ... with no hint of bitterness."

The intense golden color of this tea is mesmerizing. Surely, I muse, consuming something of such exceptional luminosity would heal all sorts of ancient ills and heartache. It is a color so brilliant one wonders if it is radiating light. Perhaps it was an oolong similar to this that inspired Dr. Kaempfer to name tea after the goddess of light. Formosa oolongs are sometimes referred to as the "Champagne of Teas," and it is easy to see why once you taste them. They often have that sparkly, bright and lively quality of what I call a "vertical tea," where the initial floral experience is so overwhelming that it goes right to my head, up into my sinus, like bubbles. It also presents those open, spacious sensations that champagnes do.

Once, early in my training, I tasted forty to sixty cups of Anxi County Tieguanyins over a two-day period. The fragrance of the oolong permeated not only my clothes but also the entire teahouse. At night, I took home piles of the spent leaves, put them on flat cookie sheets, and slowly dried them in an open oven. My whole apartment filled with the aroma as well. It turned me off to all oolongs for years. My friends argued, "There are other oolongs in the world, Frank," so I flirted with the Phoenix oolongs, the Wu Yi Yan Chas, and the old bush Shui Xians, but nothing grabbed me. Nothing soothed or comforted me until I was introduced to the Formosa oolongs. I was lucky. The embodiment of three Oriental Beauties came into my life bearing gifts from Taiwan and steered my ship back into the deep waters of the eternal feminine. Even the Tieguanyins from Taiwan were supernatural, dark moon goddesses of Pallas Athene. Guan Yin (Kuan Yin) and Thea herself summoned me to partake of my own primordial wisdom.

Oolongs can offer a middle way between the light, creative heaven, and the dark, receptive earth, between the white teas and the black. It is my hope that their popularity is a portent for the re-emergence of respect for the feminine.

There are many factors that contribute to one's tea-tasting experience. The primary variable is the individual; the secondary variable is the tea. Everyone's physiology is different. Some people simply have more taste buds per square inch and can pick up more subtle and complex notes. This may also be true for the olfactory receptors in the nose. Some people seem to have a better sense of smell than others.

Also, mouth chemistry changes from hour to hour, depending on what you put into your mouth. At a tea tasting, if you are clearing your palate or spitting the tea out after every sip, you are depleting your saliva, thus changing the natural mix of saliva and tea. Each expectoration and each sip of tea changes your mouth chemistry. If you are swallowing the tea, it is altering more than just your mouth. It is heightening all of your senses.

As it cools, the taste of tea changes, too. It continues to oxidize, even infuse to some degree.

It may not always be the taste of a tea that keeps me coming back to it, nor the taste that brings me to tears, but how that tea affects my soul, how it stirs me, how it sings in my heart, how it unravels its own stories. Sometimes the experience of a tea outweighs its taste.

The skills of a professional tea taster seem impressive. But tea tasters aren't necessarily connoisseurs. What they are looking for is consistency in the taste of their corporation's most popular teas. They are not looking for the best-tasting tea.

Tea tasters have their own jargon to evaluate tea, and are often required to articulate their experience with each tea. Though I am not a professional tea taster employed by a large corporation, I have been on a panel of judges at different juried competitions. Instead of giving a verbal description, I had to fill out a scorecard that rated the teas 1 to 10 in a number of categories and then asked for comment. Here's a sample:

Leaf Appearance Dry:	1 2 3 4 5 6 7 8 9 10
Leaf Aroma Dry:	1 2 3 4 5 6 7 8 9 10
Leaf Aroma Damp:	1 2 3 4 5 6 7 8 9 10
Smooth	
Sharp	
Delicate	
Rich	
Sweet	
Bitter	
Smoky	
Floral	
Fruity	
Leafy	
Leaf Appearance Steeping:	1 2 3 4 5 6 7 8 9 10
Liquor Aroma Steeping:	1 2 3 4 5 6 7 8 9 10
Liquor Color:	1 2 3 4 5 6 7 8 9 10
Liquor Clarity:	1 2 3 4 5 6 7 8 9 10
Liquor Taste:	1 2 3 4 5 6 7 8 9 10
Smooth	
Sharp	
Delicate	
Rich	
Sweet	
Bitter	
Smoky	
Floral	
Fruity	
Leafy	
Leaf Appearance Wet:	1 2 3 4 5 6 7 8 9 10
Leaf Aroma Wet:	1 2 3 4 5 6 7 8 9 10
Aftertaste:	1 2 3 4 5 6 7 8 9 10
Comment:	

The language of the palate is the same as it would be for the connoisseurship of any food or beverage—be it coffee, tea, chocolate, or wine. There's the "nose" or bouquet, the fragrance of the tea before you taste it. A few drops of hot water sprinkled on the dry leaves at the bottom of your brewing vessel will yield its bouquet, so will moistening the dry leaves with your breath.

The first taste of the tea at the front of the mouth is called the entry, then there's the mid-palate—the bulk of the tasting experience. It is followed by the finish, what's picked up by the taste buds at the back of the mouth, specifically in the soft palate, the pharynx, and the epiglottis.

One of my favorite descriptions of a tea was written by Roy Fong about his Oriental Beauty, Imperial Bai Hao Oolong: "This tea's elegantly twisted leaves and plentiful silver tips infuse to a pale, champagne-gold liquor with a rich, sweet, peachy perfume and delicate, full bodied, honey-kissed flavor which lasts through numerous captivating infusions." I also liked his description of his Imperial Dragon Well: "On top of the sweet, fresh, floral opening, there is a slight hint of lemon. The mid-palate is smooth, balanced, and complex, with mineral, grassy, and slightly nutty qualities."

Donald Wallis of the American Tea Masters Association invokes the taste of a tea by transporting us to its origins:

> In the early spring high Himalaya mountain mist, along steep winding well-trod paths, tea artisans clad in colorful native dress, ascend to pluck the year's most delicate leaf buds shyly emerging on the verdant terraces. Amid the crisp refreshing air and breathtaking vistas, adept hands deftly select and carefully pluck from the dew-laden bushes the prize downy shoots destined for the connoisseur's cup. As the warming sun skips across the roof of the world playfully chasing its own shadows from one soaring snowy peak to another, the baskets begin to fill and the fragrance of the freshly plucked leaf buds perfumes the terrace. An atmosphere of urgency quickens the pace and soon the brimming baskets are gathered up for the descent to the processing house far below. The freshly picked leaves are spread

onto a priceless royal carpet shimmering in a dazzling array of brilliant blue hues under shaded arbors. The withering process is precisely gauged to perfectly express the balanced sweet essence of the region's renowned Darjeeling-style flavor. While the leaves are meticulously fashioned to exemplify the beauty that deliciously blossoms into one of the world's rarest and most flavorful works of art, Himalaya Hao Cha.

Whether your predilection is to use the universal language of the trade or a more creative, romantic, or poetic vocabulary, the bottom line for the non-professional is quite simply whether or not you like the taste of the tea. Lu Yu makes a very curious comment. He says: "Its goodness is a decision for the mouth to make." At least this is the interpretation by Francis Ross Carpenter. But this line also has been translated: "Discrimination between good and bad tea is a matter for secret oral transmission." I have often pondered the meaning of "secret oral transmission." It could be that the knowledge of tea is imparted by the spoken word in the oral tradition of Taoism, from master to master, master to student, on down. Knowledge may also be transmitted sensually direct from the tea plant itself, the plant kingdom. or even the earth in the course of tasting. Or, as in my experience, the tea may put us in such an open and altered space that transmissions occur from the spirit world.

In the end, I am not interested in a chemical breakdown of the mystical experience or a neurological explanation of rapture. Everything I need to know is in the cup. There is no one constituent or agent within the leaf that stands out to give a tea its character or taste; tea is a tightly woven community. You cannot distill a tea down to its basic parts nor extract its nature without destroying that community. They all work together as a whole. They all supplement each other. One of tea's many mysteries is the perfection of its balance.

I have learned that tea, like any plant, can share with us her deepest mysteries if we ask her guidance and counsel. These secret transmissions may not even come to us until our cups are empty, for there is a teatime that begins long after our pots are cold.

Often when I'm done with tea I will continue to sit in this space I've created for myself, feeling energy moving about in my body, feeling things shift and tension release. I will try to yield to each knock or curious turn she generates. The moments of tension are actual places of physical discomfort I associate with the effects of caffeine. I'll feel tightness gathering around my heart. I focus attention on my heart, open it, and the tension goes away. As the tension shifts, I may have to do this several times at differing locations in my body until I find balance.

Tea has a way of softening us, making us vulnerable and receptive. If we take the time and continue to sit quietly in our chairs, savoring the taste and the moment, we may remember not only where we mislaid our spectacles but also where we have mislaid our dreams.

Camellia
A Hymn From St. Camellia's Church of the First Infusion

VI

CAMELLIA: THE BOTANY OF TEA

FOR 250 YEARS the botanical name for tea was *Thea sinensis*. It was changed to *Camellia sinensis* around 1956. Why it was changed is not altogether clear. Plant names change from time to time as taxonomic criteria for defining a plant become more and more refined. A friend of mine put it well when he said that the very formal rules of taxonomy simply caught up with tea. I have noticed that the only place where tea retains its original name of *Thea sinensis* is in homeopathic *materia medicas*.

Now it is fashionable to declare that there is only one species of tea, *Camellia sinensis*, and that there are many varietals and cultivars within this species. A varietal is a naturally occurring variety of a plant, and cultivars are man made or horticulturally derived.

The word *Camellia* comes from the Moravian Jesuit missionary and botanist, Georg Josef Kamel (1661–1700) who first described the plant. Tea bushes are directly related to the flowering Camellia bushes (*Camellia japonica*) that we see growing in the warmer parts of the United States.

The word *sinensis* is Latin (*sino*) for China.

Both of these Camellias (*sinensis* and *japonica*) are from the Theaceae family, which contains forty genera. One of these forty genera is the genus *Camellia*, which houses about 280 species. It is the species *C. sinensis* we call "tea." In other words, all tea is made from a single species of plant, *C. sinensis*!

In the past ten to twenty years, it was thought that there were several species of tea. Chief among them were the small-leafed *C. sinensis* of China and the large leafed *C. assamica* of India. In Yunnan province, China, however, there is also a large-leafed *dai yeh* variety very similar to the Assam leaf. When you look at a map you can see that Chinese and Indian teas are separated only by one-hundred-mile stretch of Burma. What Yunnan has that Assam does not have are tea trees thousands of years old. It has also been suggested that there are many more naturally occurring varietals in Yunnan than in Assam.

Tracking the botany may seem complicated because there are rival factions of botanists. The "lumpers" want to lump certain species under one roof. The "splitters" want to subdivide a species into numerous species.

The name Thea was bestowed upon tea by a Dr. Engelbert Kaempfer in the early 1700s. In Greek, *thea* and *theo* mean goddess or god, and *Thea sinensis* means Goddess of China. Thea, or Theia, herself, is a renowned pre-Hellenic goddess of light and luminaries. In Greek mythology, she is the daughter of Uranus (her father, the Greek representation of heaven or the sky) and Ga, or Gaia (mother earth). The daughter of heaven and earth, you might say. Thea's husband is Hyperion. Between them they had three daughters—Eos, Aurora, and Selene—and a son, Helios. Astrologically, Thea is said to be the daughter of the wise centaur Chiron. While there is some dispute as to whether Dr. Kaempfer knew any of this mythology, there is no doubt in my mind. I would even bet that Thea herself ventured into his study one night to plant the name.

THEA
Who is this woman that makes me sneak out at night and stay up way beyond my means?
Who is this woman for whom I labor longer days that I might buy her things: porcelain and jade, linen, and silver?
Who is this woman for whom I forfeit money meant for food?
If I could dress her in silk, I would!

Tea is a broad-leafed evergreen much like oleanders and rhododendrons, though unrelated. The unusual thing about tea is that it blossoms and sets fruit in the fall. In tea gardens, it is prevented from blossoming by using fertilizers that enhance leaf production. A fertilizer high in nitrogen will force a plant to put out a lot of green but not to flower. The practice of physically removing flowers from the tea bush by hand to promote leaf growth is not out of the question, either. Roy Fong will tell you that if the tea plant is well tended—well trimmed, well fed, and watered—the plant will flower less, since it is living well and doesn't feel the need to pass on its genes. The point is to put all of the plant's energy, its vital forces, into the leaf.

Not all varietals of *C. sinensis* can make a decent cup of tea, however. Some are best left as ornamental shrubs and are sold as such.

The other interesting aspect of tea is that it has what botanists call "perfect flowers" or male and female reproductive organs in the same flower (monoecious). It is self-pollinating.

The part of the tea bush that is harvested are the buds at the very ends of the branches and the first and second leaves after that bud. By buds I mean leaf buds, not flower buds.

Tea can grow from sea level to elevations as high as 8,200 feet. Some of the highest plantations are in the Nilgiri Hills of southern India. People grow tea at tea stations in such diverse climes as Hawaii, Oregon, England, and the Azores, and some of it is quite exceptional.

The China plant seems to have originated in a very specific area of central Asia bordered by four countries: southeastern Tibet; northern Burma, or Myanmar; India, particularly the state of Assam; and China in Yunnan and Sichuan provinces. Through this region run some of the world's most legendary river systems: the Brahmaputra, the Irrawaddy, the Salween, the Mekong, and the Yangtze. This is an intense area of plunging gorges and towering mountains. At one point the Yangtze and the Mekong are separated by just fifty miles of mountains, as are the Mekong and the Salween at another point. The headwaters of all these rivers rise in the Tibetan Himalayas.

Within this region, China has long claimed to be tea's homeland. Most people I know give the nod to China, but the truth is nobody really knows. There is certainly no other country in the area where tea is so deeply woven into the rich fabric of its ancient history, cultural traditions, and folklore as in China. The very word *tea* is Chinese, from the Amoy dialect.

The strongest case for China as the homeland builds on the fact that within this terrain, bordered by these four countries, is a region of extraordinarily dense vegetation and biodiversity. This region is in Yunnan and Sichuan provinces. Here the Hengduan Mountains, the southernmost mountain range in this area, were thought to have inhibited the flow of the last great glaciers 14,000 years ago. They provided a refuge for many plants and animals. The April 2002 edition of *National Geographic* cites 3,500 different kinds of plants here, including 230 species of rhododendrons and 50 species of conifers. Roses are thought to have originated here as well. Only recently has China become acutely aware of its treasure, scrambling to create dozens of national parks and reserves in the region, according to the article.

Humanity's first encounter with the tea plant is lost in antiquity. The most popular Chinese story places that initial meeting in 2,737 B.C. Sheng Nong, the legendary emperor of China at the time, also known as the Divine Husbandman, was in a wooded glade boiling water to drink when a tea leaf fell into his pot from a nearby tree. He immediately noticed the invigorating properties of the leaf. The details of the story differ but you can bet that 2,737 B.C. was an auspicious year in the Chinese astrological calendar. "Who indeed," says Francis Ross Carpenter, in his introduction to his translation of Lu Yu's, *Classic of Tea*, "other than this Divine, conceived by a princess under the influence of the dragon, could have given tea to the world?"

However as any ethnobotanist will tell you, it is far more accurate to push that first encounter back many hundreds of thousands of years to when ancient humans were dependent upon their knowledge of plants for survival. They needed to know which plants were harmful and which, beneficial. It is believed that ancient man first chewed raw tea leaves from wild trees.

Even though it is such a simple plant, there aren't many people that know much about it. It can be a frustrating experience tracking down tea botanists to get answers to specific questions about the botany, cultivation, and harvesting of tea. One question that continues to confound me: Is there a specific botanical name for plants, like tea, that blossom only in the fall?

Here is the traditional taxonomic classification of tea. Note the changes to the system since 1936, when William Ukers published his two-volume treatise *All About Tea*.

Ukers 1936	*Encyclopedia Britannica 2005 edition*
kingdom: plant	kingdom: plant
subkingdom: none	subkingdom: tracheobionta
division: angiospermae	division: magnoliophyta
class: dicotyledone	class: magnoliopsida
subclass: dilleniidae	subclass: dilleniidae
order: parietals	order: theales
family: Theaceae	family: Theaceae
genus: Thea	genus: Camellia
species: sinensis	species: sinensis
variety: sinensis	variety: sinensis

As technological advances split hairs over certain species, science will continue to refine how plants are classified. I'm sure that with time, we'll see further changes in tea's taxonomic breakdown.

VII

THE DIVERGENT WATERS OF THE STREAM

Water flows from high in the mountains.
Water runs deep in the earth.
Miraculously, water comes to us and sustains all life!
—*Thich Nhat Hanh*

All things return to soul through water.
—*Steven Eisenstadt*

A FRIEND OF MINE used to say that if you want to get to know a place and its people drink the water. Water carries with it the temperament of the rock within which it rests. It also carries all the minerals of the soil through which it passes to get to that resting place. Even if you filter the water or boil it first before you consume it, there is still something that may be discerned from the local water, something that the water transmits to its people.

Water is susceptible to a great many subtle influences. It is particularly susceptible to prayer. Any of you that have read the books of Masaru Emoto know this to be true. Mr. Emoto demonstrates the effects of prayer on water and actually photographs the results. I always pray over my water before I use it. This "raises the vibration" of the water and makes for a better tasting cup. I also pray over the brewing leaves because I know that spiritualizing one's tea changes its leaf chemistry.

Tea is mostly water. It is easy to get sidetracked by a study of water just as it is easy to over-focus on the study of tea and forget that what we're interested in is their union. Sometimes I muse about placing several types of water next to the dry leaves I've selected and having Miss Camellia choose her own mate through some intuitive divination.

The type of water you choose to make your tea will determine its taste. The bottled water you drink may taste great by itself but it may not necessarily make a good pot of tea. You don't want water with too much taste or personality because it will inhibit, overshadow, or upstage your tea. Try this experiment: Make yourself two cups of tea using two different kinds of water. Use tap water for one and purified water for the other and note the taste difference. It can be dramatic. The tap water can make your tea taste flat and boring, and the purified water may make your tea a lot more flavorful and interesting.

The subject of water can be a science unto itself, a very fascinating science. The bottom line is always going to be up to you. Part of the fun is experimenting with different kinds of water to see which makes the best cup for your particular palate.

We are very fortunate to live in a time when we have at our disposal a vast array of waters with which to make tea: bottled spring waters from all over the globe; distilled and de-ionized (DI) water; water that has been molecularly rearranged; and water that has been purified with charcoal, ultra-violet radiation, electromagnetic radiation, reverse osmosis membranes, etc.

I'd like to share some of my water exploits with you because I ended up settling in a very unlikely place in my choice of tea water.

Here at 7,000 feet in the mountains of north central New Mexico our tap water contains about 400 parts per million (ppm) of total dissolved solids (tds). If you accidentally sprayed your windows with this water, the glass would be covered with white spots. This water is useless for tea! It has to be brought through a reverse osmosis (RO) membrane to bring the tds down to a certain acceptable marriageable eligibility, about 20–40 tds, some say. You can honor tea by seeking out the best possible water for it to marry. It may take some effort, but think of this marriage as a sacrament.

Once I did a three-day water fast with the intention of discerning the best water for my tea. At the end of that fast my palate and my whole body had become abnormally refined and sensitized. I found the water I most preferred to drink straight did not suit my tea. I had over-focused on the water and not on the union, the marriage of the water and the tea.

We do not live in a perfect world where local spring water is pure and not contaminated with acid rain or parasites like giardia. We do not live in China, where we can use the very water in which the tea bush itself sinks its roots. One of my first teachers used what he called "steam distilled, re-mineralized water." He basically created his own. He steam distilled his water then added a splash of local spring water.

Lu Yu, of course, preferred water from mountain streams or spring water, but Lu Yu was not China's only tea master. Other masters used rainwater or melted snow, which is basically distilled water.

In Mr. Ukers' book *All About Tea* we read: "Some experts have made a practice of using distilled water for testing. While such a method will invariably discover the intrinsic qualities of tea, it will not guide a taster in the choice of tea that will be perfectly suitable to the water of a certain district in which the tea is to be sold." What are we trying to discover if not tea's intrinsic qualities?

I have heard people describe distilled water as dead and flat. The same could be said for water that comes out of your tap. You shouldn't have to do soul retrieval work on a water to make it usable. If distilled water is all you have, boil it. This will liven it up a bit by re-oxygenating it.

Steam-distilled water is so oxygen lacking that it will corrode a pipe. It will strip from the pipe oxygen molecules it needs as it seeks homeostasis. De-ionized water is not steam distilled and is, thus, not so oxygen lacking and not so flat tasting. On the DI water dispensers in organic grocery stores we often read that it is good for brewing herbal teas. It is also good for people on certain cleansing and/or fasting diets. While it may extract minerals and nutrients from our bodies it also extracts toxins. The aggressive nature of distilled and de-ionized water is neutralized during the brewing process. By the time we drink our tea, the water has lost its ability to pull minerals and toxins from our bodies.

I use de-ionized water that I buy in five-gallon bottles at a local bulk water distributor. What it lacks in mineral content it makes up for in its aggressive leeching capacities. I know of no other water that coaxes from the leaf all of tea's most subtle nuances. Refined water for refined leaves, I say!

HYDRATION AND DEHYDRATION

Sometimes what I desire is water, not tea. And when I heed my body's call for water, and have a tall glass or two, I feel just as invigorated.

The problem with water is that we never seem to get enough of it. Once I sent away to a large tea corporation for their tea information packet and on the very top of that pile was a pamphlet on dehydration.

Tea is beguiling. On one hand, it can hydrate you. On the other hand, because it contains three diuretics, it can dehydrate you as well. Here in the desert we have to pay very close attention to the water that we lose. Chronic inattentiveness to our body's need for water can cause all kinds of problems, and the symptoms of dehydration are insidious. It can lower blood pressure as well as make us dizzy and light headed. I get headaches when my body is low on water so I try to remember to replace the fluids that I lose especially when I'm drinking tea. Instead of reaching for an aspirin for the headache, I just have water.

Tea is mostly water and so are we. We may all be much more thirsty than we think. Why not begin by self-medicating with water before we reach for something else.

VIII

HANGCHOW HARRY'S BAR AND GRILL

AFTER AN EXASPERATING DAY in Hangzhou trying to get some legal papers translated, I went over to Harry's.

"Give me a double Dian Hong with a Puerh chaser!"

"Hard day?" Harry asked. I said nothing, didn't even look up, and he disappeared.

When Harry returned he put a cup down in front of me and said, "Here, try some of this!"

"What is it?" I asked.

"A Tang dynasty tea!" he answered.

I was pleasantly surprised. "Where'd you get this?"

"The Tea Research Institute!" He smiled.

"Oh!" Harry had connections. He wasn't one of those imposing, pontificating personalities you'd find trying to sell their wares.

"It's a curious thing how often a tea merchant resembles his teas," Harry said. "I remember one guy—all fluff and no substance. His teas turned out to be exactly the same way, boring and faceless."

"I'm more interested in what the tea has to say than what the man has to say about the tea," I said.

Harry nodded. "If a merchant doesn't have a sophisticated palate, you can bet he's not going to have any sophisticated teas."

I thought about the ten China tea samples I had ordered from a well-known tea company in California. When I laid them out side by side, I noticed immediately that not a single one had a finished quality. I found out later that the tea was bought from farmers *on their way* to the factory where the leaves would have been finished for a nominal fee! Simply because someone sells tea doesn't make him an authority or a connoisseur.

As people started coming into the bar, I moved to a chair by a window looking out across West Lake. There, sitting at a small table at the water's edge were three striking elderly gentlemen. Their long flowing robes with voluminous sleeves, hair tied up in a knot atop their heads, and their long beards were reminiscent of the Tang era, yet here they were drinking tea.

The first was a rather intimidating figure, stern and forbidding. Yet the more I watched him the softer he became, softer and wise. He possessed a depth and wisdom I could not fathom.

The second and most animated of the three did most of the talking. The others listened intently, as if mesmerized by his words. He'd obviously been drinking too much, whether tea or wine I do not know.

The third gentleman was the one brewing and serving tea. It appeared the others were quite pleased with his technique. Watching him for a while, I, too, could see that he was no ordinary tea man.

"Who are these guys, Harry?" I called out, without taking my eyes off them. But before Harry got to my table all three were swallowed up in a mist that suddenly enshrouded the lake.

I must have looked white as a sheet when Harry got to my table. Funny how when you think you've seen a ghost, you end up looking like one—pale, transfigured, otherworldly.

"You okay?" he asked.

"I'll take some more of that tea!" I heard myself say.

I dreamed of those three gentlemen that night. But this time they appeared in a different constellation, so that I could identify each one. They were the Taoist Immortal, Lu Tung Pin; China's famous poet, Li Po (Li Bai); and China's patron saint of tea, Lu Yu.

POETRY FOR LI PO

LINES OF AFFECTION FOR A TANG DYNASTY POET

I poured myself another cup of Wu Yi Bao Zhong and watched winter ravens drift in the deep mountain azure. Coyotes wove in and out of my tea trance, and into this dream Li Po appeared atop a white doe and beckoned, ascending a distant peak. When I awoke my tea had iced over.

I half expect to see
The lips of this celestial soul
Kiss the calm surface of my tea
When o'er my head,
The liquor raised,
I gaze up through that glass gaiwan
Offering my first sip to you.

Dragon clouds pass before the moon
And I think of Li Po
Alone and drunk
In some wooded glade
Far, far away

Passed out on the moss of a northern tree,
A cold wind shifts along the ground
Freezing the tears on your face
Tears of loneliness.

Old friend,
Let us meet at Da Hong Pao pagoda,
Warm our hands at coal fired braziers
And warm our bellies with the dark canyon's tea.

Perhaps something of Li Po
Did enter the Yangtze
When, as the story says, he entered

By way of the moon.
Who could tell me?

If a pearl is formed when moonlight enters an oyster
Then perhaps something of Li Po
Is held by the crystals found on the river's floor.

IX

A NIGHT OF HEAVY DRINKING, OR TEA-FRIED BRAIN

"Use you own batteries!" said the tea plant. "Don't use mine!"

A FRIEND OF MINE used to say, "Teatime is an oasis of civility in a world gone mad," but tea is not exempt from its own world of madness! You go through life and meet someone and think quietly to yourself, "Gee, he drinks too much." Further on down the road, you meet someone else and you think quietly to yourself, "Gee, he doesn't drink enough."

Tea books never address the difficulties some people have with caffeine, or the fun, for that matter. It can be a complex issue and a very personal one.

The most honest account of a negative caffeine experience is the one M.F.K. Fisher shares in her introduction to James Norwood Pratt's *Tea Lover's Treasury*. She describes a drunken tannic fog that overtook her after three hours of drinking tea with friends. It was an episode that so deeply shook her she never had tea again. At one point, Ms. Fisher writes: "Did I find myself high drunk on fury and frustration, or on other chemicals like caffeine?" Ms. Fisher was like me, extremely sensitive to caffeine.

Once your body seizes up in a toxic reaction to this drug you never forget it. Once you've been pummeled by excessive amounts of caffeine, it can open a Pandora's Box of powerful emotions you may not know you possessed. Personally, I become more than a little irritable. I can only have tea once a day!

I think we've all had experiences of having ingested too much tea and, like Ms. Fisher, had to breathe through it, so to speak, and ride it out.

I have never been comfortable clothing my experiences of tea in the language of insobriety as others do. Intemperance, yes, but not drunkenness. Overindulgence in tea does not diminish or impair my faculties as with alcohol; it enhances them. There are sensations that we may equate with being drunk if we have no other language for it, but the altered state produced by tea has an entirely different spin on it. Explore it for yourself!

Tea is psychoactive; it affects the mental processes by quickening the mind. It is also psychotropic because it can alter our perceptions, emotions, and our behavior. It is consciousness-raising. "What's that?" a young man once asked actress Lily Tomlin during her "Works in Progress" tour. "Something women do!" she retorted.

Like other consciousness-expanding substances, tea heightens all of our senses, not just our rudimentary ones. Tea deepens awareness of things around us. The veil separating us from the spirit world grows thinner, and we begin to feel kinship with all life. Some teas even appear to come with an attendant spirit when two or more people gather in her name. As technology becomes more and more sophisticated, science may begin to detect even more subtle energies at play in tea and how it affects us.

Every tea is a remedy of one sort or another. What some teas don't heal, others will. There are even teas that balance the ill affects of other teas. Tea may also heal us of things we did not know we had.

We don't think of tea as being the world's most popular anti-depressant but it is. Both tea and anti-depressants have unique places in today's society. Tea, however, is a lot safer than the pharmaceuticals on the market. None of the side effects. None of the arduous struggle to wean yourself off of them when you no longer need them.

I took the antidepressant Lexapro for a year and a half once, and it took what seemed forever to get off of it. I actually learned more about my own depression coming off of Lexapro than I did when I was on it. I must say that the drug did what it was supposed to do, though. It created an alternate channel for me to go down when depression came on. It sort of short-circuited the old synapses and created new ones that brought me to different places. For example, a couple of times, while on the drug, I permitted myself to drop down into a very deep state of depression that was unfamiliar to me. It was unfamiliar to me because it was not depression. It was grief. I had always identified it as depression because I'd never really hung out there for any period of time to figure out that there might be something else going on. It was quite a realization. Depression was not the last chamber in my journey of descent. It was only a doorway. Once I got to grief, I could "run it through my body," let it rip, and be done with it. The odd thing is that I didn't want to be done with it. Once the grief had subsided, I found myself in such an extraordinary place of peace and wisdom in my body that I didn't want to leave. I could access places of knowledge in myself that I had long forgotten about. Places of knowing. Places of trust. This is the pelvic floor. The "bottom" of my being. The place my soul had been calling out for me to reclaim and re-inhabit.

I was reminded of a passage from Rainer Maria Rilke: "Perhaps all the dragons of our lives are princesses who are only waiting to see us once beautiful and brave. Perhaps everything terrible is in its deepest being something helpless that wants help from us...then that which now still seems to us the most alien will become what we most trust and find most faithful."

Tea often takes me to those deep places within my soul, but I also know how to get there on my own. This is important because when we start relying (too much) on things outside of ourselves to get us places, we can trip ourselves up. Fortunately, tea is not an herb that trips me up.

Tea was Ms. Fisher's poison, and so it is for many people. A friend of mine suggests there are three groups of people that caffeine affects differently: those for whom caffeine acts as a poison, those that have no problem with it at all, and those for whom it is a medicine.

The primary healing benefits of tea are not attributed to caffeine, but then it depends on what type of healing you're talking about. There are healings that affect our physical body, our emotional body, and our spiritual body. We read a lot about diets these days but not much about mental and emotional diets. It is not only what we put into our bodies that creates "dis-ease," it is also what we put into our hearts (what we permit ourselves to feel) and what we put into our minds (what we permit ourselves to think). If you are struggling under the weight of an absolutely black mood there is a great deal to be said about the power of caffeine to resurrect you.

There is a lot more chemistry—and mythology—going on in a cup of tea than just the caffeine. There are two other stimulants, theobromine and theophyline; a relaxant, L-theanine; and all the polyphenols, catechins, flavonols, flavonoids, etc.

The scientific arena has contributed greatly to our knowledge and understanding of tea but the problem is science tends to over-focus on tea's individual constituents, rather than how those individual constituents work together in the community of the leaf. Tea is more than the sum of its parts. The authors of *The World of Caffeine* write that "caffeine comes to us accompanied by delights beyond its power to intoxicate: the sensual appeal of its most commonly enjoyed vehicles, coffee, tea, and chocolate." Part of that sensuality is, of course, the alluring tastes of these substances. The authors also write: "Coffee and tea contain so many pharmacologically active substances that there is no easy way to isolate the effects of caffeine from those of the other substances they contain."

There are three distinct problems to consider when talking about caffeine: one, the scientific research on caffeine is incomplete and inconclusive; two, because everyone's constitutions are different, everyone responds and reacts to caffeine differently (Some say this is directly related to blood type.); and three, again, we tend to over-focus on caffeine itself and not on the entire community in which it is engaged and interacting.

Caffeine stimulates the secretion of the hormone adrenaline. The more tea I drink, the more adrenaline I have coursing through my veins. This puts me into a "fight or flight" mode that is very uncomfortable and feels out of control.

If you're already in that mode, any substance containing caffeine can push you right over the edge. Or, if you are very sensitive, you just have to watch it. A caffeine headache lasts about a day when I stop imbibing. If I wean myself off gradually, I have no headache at all. What is more challenging to deal with, of course, is the physical and emotional let-down, that "sinking feeling" that causes us to make tea in the first place.

Some people say that tea is addictive. But the word addiction has so many negative connotations in our society today that I hesitate to use it in reference to tea. It is, therefore, not my intention to present tea as an addictive substance, but rather as a boon, an ally, that helps us become better and more sensitive human beings.

Lu Yu was so concerned about overindulgence in tea that he forewarns us twice in the first three pages of his book. He writes that the injurious properties of tea are not unlike those of ginseng. So what do we know about those adverse effects? We know that consuming excessive amounts of ginseng can cause high blood pressure, insomnia, diarrhea, and dizziness. The best advice I can give is the advice given by Lu Yu, China's patron saint of tea: "Moderation is the very essence of tea."

If you are conflicted about your use of tea or worry about getting addicted, tea could present a problem. Often, however, it is not the substance we are addicted to but the state that substance produces.

Even though tea's botanical name was changed to *Camelia sinensis* in the 1950s, we still find her original name of *Thea* intact elsewhere. *Thea* dwells among tea's lesser-known stimulants theobromine ("food of the gods") and theophyline ("leaf of the gods"), and in tea's relaxant, L-theanine, as well as in the botanical name for the family of tea, Theaceae.

Tea was named after the goddess Thea for good reason, but as anthropologist Marija Gimbutas points out in her books, the role of the goddess is not all love and light. She is not only life giving but also death wielding. "Many alkaloids present a double face," say the authors of *The World of Caffeine*, "exhibiting both poisonous and curative properties." In other words, some of us cannot afford even the most meager flirtation with this lady because of her ability to waken us from perhaps more than we wish to be awakened from. Caffeine can be, for the more delicate among us, the tempest in the teacup.

What I've found is that I may learn just as much about tea from having it as from not having it at all. I start feeling run down if I've been drinking tea for several months without a break. Drinking a lot of tea taxes the adrenals, the glands that secrete adrenaline, and makes me feel exhausted. Once the adrenals are overtaxed they start drawing on the other glands in the endocrine system, the thyroid and the pituitary in particular. This can be problematic if you have hypothyroidism, as I do; my thyroid begins to swell up and hurt. Another symptom of adrenal fatigue is not being able to stay awake, no matter how much tea you've consumed.

If I feel I've been reaching for tea too often or inappropriately, I will stop for a while and "detox." By "detox" I mean I stop having tea for a week or two to clear out all the residual caffeine. I give my body time to rest, to catch up with itself. If my inclination is to have another cup of tea when I'm feeling low, I find it wise to ask myself, what kind of low is it? What's the tone and texture of this low? Is it simply because I have low blood sugar and need something to eat? Am I dehydrated and need water? Or is it the sluggishness related to low thyroid or overtaxed adrenals, in which case I need to "feed my thyroid" with foods high in iodine, like kelp.

If I have been somewhat over exuberant with my libations, there are also several tinctures and remedies that are helpful for caffeine overload. The homeopathic remedy *coffea cruda* (that's right, it's potentized coffee) acts as an aid for insomnia. Homeopathic *chamomilla* helps with irritability. So does good ol' chamomile tea. The adaptogen, Siberian ginseng (a different plant than the popular Korean ginseng) helps the body maintain balance or homeostasis. The amino acid, L-theanine, or Suntheanine, which the Japanese synthesized from green tea, is not only the relaxing agent in tea, it also antidotes caffeine to some extent. Homeopathic *thyroidinum* is quite effective in relieving thyroid stress, and licorice tea helps support the adrenal glands.

I have also found that the homeopathic remedy potentized from tea, *Thea sinensis*, has brought me much relief. On an acute level, it has helped me with insomnia and headaches, particularly caffeine headaches. It has also stabilized me in moments of unrestrained partying, tea partying that is, by *antidoting* the more challenging aspects of excessive tea ingestion. In the long run it has afforded me moments of profound balance, moments of calm and clarity, as if it were an adaptogen.

You would be hard pressed, however, to find a homeopath who has ever prescribed *Thea sinensis*. This is because the symptoms for which it is recommended do not often constellate together. In fact, the symptoms are polar opposites, ranging from euphoria, exaltation, and ecstasy to aggressive impulses and violent rage. Tea has the capacity to relax and stimulate beyond our comfort level.

It is the other end of the spectrum that is more troubling: feeling like you could hurt someone. Rather extreme, but real. I have run the gamut, just from the ingestion of too much tea!

Homeopaths forewarn their patients to avoid certain foods that will antidote a remedy, such as garlic, camphor, menthol, mint, coffee, and marijuana. Some say these agents distract our bodies from the subtle healing frequency a remedy needs to effect a cure, and that they create imbalance in the body at a time when we need stability to heal. Other homeopaths suggest that there may be a chemical used in the processing of coffee that's the culprit. One homeopath even said that extreme emotional states will antidote a remedy, requiring a second dosage. For years I was under the impression that for a homeopathic remedy to work, all foods with caffeine should be avoided. But this is not the case. Tea passes muster, and so does chocolate.

Over the years I've read articles about the caffeine levels in different types of teas. Some say it's all pretty much the same. Some say it depends on the amount of leaf you use and how long you brew. Some even claim white teas appear to have no caffeine in them at all. Personally, I've noticed that white and green teas have the least, black teas have the most, and oolongs are somewhere in the middle. Sometimes I make a white tea for myself to help counter the ill effects of a particularly strong Puerh. From my own point of view, no matter how strong I make my tea, it's still going to contain less caffeine than coffee, even if the color of the liquor is just as black. For most people caffeine is quite benign. Fortunately for us sensitive ones, it doesn't take long before we know how much is enough.

Since caffeine is highly soluble in water, it is easy to decaffeinate your own tea. Simply let your leaves or teabags steep in hot water for anywhere from forty to sixty seconds, throw off that first infusion and re-steep the tea with fresh hot water. You will lose some of the flavor but will have decaffeinated your tea by approximately 80%. The temperature of the water you decaffeinate with should be the same temperature you intend to brew with.

I did not come to all of these remedies for caffeine overload in a single evening. It took years. Initially, I'd stay up all night, walking over San Francisco's many hills, drinking a lot of water to help flush my system, eating a heavy meal to help absorb the caffeine, and perhaps, stopping by Li Po's Bar on Grant before attempting to retire. Li Po never showed!

Once I had the opportunity to participate in a five-day tea intensive in San Francisco. At one point we were drinking forty to sixty cups of various Tekuanyins over two ten-hour days. At the close of that second day my teacher noticed I was "somewhat uncomfortable." My face was white, my breathing labored, I was about to pass out. He ran out of the teahouse up to the corner grocer and brought back a huge chocolate chip cookie. "Eat this!" he commanded. The result was immediate and dramatic. My body's extreme state was instantly relieved. I became a functional human being. Thank goodness my teacher was familiar with my symptoms. He also knew I hadn't had much to eat. It wasn't necessarily the best thing to have put in my stomach, but it gave my body something to metabolize.

Overindulgence is not an experience I seek out. I know my limits now. It is sometimes challenging, however, to enter these states intentionally, in order to "check my progress." To use them as a kind of gauge, a reality check, a therapeutic tool. Most of the time these extreme states just make me feel horrible, destroy my health, and take me days to recover.

There is a famous tea poem by Lu T'ung, also known as Master Jade Spring, in which he describes his experiences drinking seven bowls of tea. At the end he writes, "The seventh cup—Ah, but I could take no more! I only feel the breath of the cool wind that rises in my sleeves." In another translation we read, "This seventh is the utmost I can drink—a light breeze issues from my armpits."

I have had many experiences of tea mobilizing the chi in my body and of it clearing out occluded meridians as it passes through. It has a different charge than just caffeine. There's something else going on. My acupuncturist says, "Tea brings up the pure chi and cleans out the damp heat. Tea helps to clean out the meridians. It helps to clear away blockages in the meridians so that energy can flow again!" In Wang Ling's *Chinese Tea Culture* the author writes, "Man's vitality lies in collateral channels that tea helps to dredge." I was talking about this at a lecture one night. Afterwards, a young couple came up to me and asked me if tea were an aphrodisiac. "It's not known for being one," I said, "but some teas can stimulate the movement of chi most anywhere in our body, especially if there's a blockage."

On several occasions I have had the sensation of an almost imperceptible breeze blowing down the sleeves of my long-sleeved shirt. I realized it was chi-related because I've had experiences of chi streaming out of the palms of my hands and the bottoms of my feet. Thank goodness we are constructed with certain pressure relief valves that kick in at pivotal moments. I wonder if the goddess Kuan Yin physically rose up to heaven from her residence on Putuo Fu Shan Island because she drank too much of that island's tea!

If you are familiar with how to move energy, or chi, around in your body, then you can choose how caffeine affects you; you don't have to be a victim of it. You can antidote the effects of caffeine by grounding underneath it. This means, one, being aware of where your energy is in your body in the first place and, two, dropping that energy down onto your pelvic floor. I usually hang out there until the jitters are gone. You can also continue to run your energy down from the pelvic floor through your legs, knees, and feet and into the ground, quite literally grounding out the effects of caffeine and grounding yourself as well.

You can practice this when you're drinking tea. You follow the warmth of the liquor down into your belly. Feel the calming, relaxing effects of the tea there, letting go as you let down into yourself. Breathe into that space you've created for yourself, and there you are. It takes a while to cultivate this "lower chamber" and the "roadway" that leads to it, but once your energy and attention are in place, you begin to notice that when the caffeine from the tea kicks in, you wake up in your belly, not in your head. Otherwise, it's easy to get busy in your head after a cup of tea or after a cup of anything with caffeine in it! I don't like the rushed and anxious feelings because I become susceptible to distractions. If there's too much going on in my head, I tend to get spaced out, ungrounded, "out of my body."

Sometimes I question my motives when I reach for tea. I know that it can be abused. I've abused it. I know that we can have a dysfunctional relationship with tea as we can with anyone or anything else. It is important not to bestow upon tea charms it does not possess, nor to give it powers greater than our own. Tea will take us as far as we are willing to go, but it is not meant to replace the resources we were born with. Tea is an ally, an aid, not a crutch.

When you're dealing with transforming the soul, you're dealing with alchemy. There are some teas that are alchemical in that they can affect (touch) our souls and help to transform us with the insights they share. One technique taught by Taoists for moving energy around in our body is called "internal alchemy" and involves a certain pathway called "the microcosmic orbit." It begins just below the naval. You focus your energy and attention (your awareness) there until you feel a warm, tingling sensation then you move on to the next point lower and deeper down in the body. The pathway drops into your bottom (the pelvic floor) then rises up the back, over the top of the head, and down the front of the body to the naval again where the cycle starts over. There are variations on the practice depending on the lineage of your instructor. Skilled practitioners may cultivate and store their chi. The Chinese have given evocative names to each point on the trajectory—names like the Jade Pillow, the Crystal Palace, Immortal Realm Peak, Heaven Rushing Out, Spiral of Rice Grains, Outer Ring of the Forest, The Soul Pavilion, Bubbling Spring. It is a "loop drive" you might say with scenic "pull outs." Refining our bodies with techniques such as these makes it easy to track the effects of a single cup of green tea—or a single thought.

Let's pull off the road for a few moments and pause at one of my favorite spots on the microcosmic orbit. There is a place in the human body that is considered sacred by both the Chinese and the ancient Greeks. The Chinese call it "the Immortal Bone." It is also called "The Passage to the Doorway of Life and Death." The Greeks call it the "sacred bone" and used this bone with its eight "holes of the soul" in sacrifices. We know it as the sacrum. The sacrum is the triangular bone composed of five fused vertebrae at the lower part of the vertebral column forming the posterior section of the pelvis. The coccyx, or tailbone, consists of the four vertebrae that are attached to the bottom of the sacrum. Because of the energetic interaction of the sacrum and the coccyx, Taoists treat them as one center on the microcosmic orbit.

It is at this point where chi enters the spinal cord from "a lake 10,000 meters deep." Or where sexual energy first enters the central nervous system and rises up the spine. I call it the pelvic floor or the wisdom body. In Latin, *pelvis* means basin. In other words, we might say that upon the floor of this basin, this receptacle rests the organs of the lower abdominal cavity.

So here we are upon "the shores of a lake that lay beyond." A lake that is surging with powerful sexual energy. Needless to say, it is easy to get distracted here. The view from the lake can be quite engaging. Kundalini energy (the coiled serpent or dragon) lies dormant (in the lake) at the base of the spine until it is activated by a specific practice.

The Chinese believe that this lake is unique in that it is spring fed from below. A "sacral pump" at the point of the coccyx and sacrum draws chi from the lake and pushes it up the spine. The Taoist Immortal, Lu Tung Pin, is associated with the first movement of energy up this channel. This sacral/coccygeal center transforms and refines not only our sexual energy but also an "earth energy" that we draw from the earth through our feet and up our back. It is a very busy place.

When man lived closer to the earth, he lived lower in his body and was more at peace. Today we tend to live higher in our bodies and are thus more susceptible to fear. When we engage with the Earth, when we invoke her wisdom and the wisdom of the plants that grow within her, our dialogue begins here in this sacred place. It is not with our mind that we engage in this dialogue, but with our bodies.

This is the place I go when I want an antidote to overindulging in caffeine. It is also where I go to access the truths my body holds. Surrendering into these spaces is an exercise in self-compassion. It is a descent! A descent into the dragon's domain. Dragons can be quite frightening to behold. We come across them from time to time when we embark upon the waters of our psyche, or feel ourselves descending into a dark night of the soul. We go down and down until we feel we've bottomed out. Then we realize there's still further to go. Finally we land on the bedrock of our own personal truth, wisdom, and faith. Dragons are all carriers of wisdom, but it is easy to forget this when we're about to be consumed by one.

Often when you see a dragon depicted in Chinese art, it is playing with a disk or ball, some say a pearl. This is the essence of the dragon. The dragon both guards the pearl and bestows it as a gift upon those who have earned it. It is almost as if the dragon were standing guard at the gates of our shadow sides. It is only by befriending the dragon, befriending our shadow, that we may be gifted with the pearl, vital life force. Thus, we see Kuan Yin standing on the back of a dragon in stormy seas, and women walking down thoroughfares with a dragon on a leash. Unlike the West, the Chinese never betrayed their relationship with the dragon. If Western man had learned to sheathe his sword and enter into the bowels of the dragon, I think he would be a very different breed. By slaying all the dragons of his past, Western man has nearly succeeded in extinguishing his soul!

Tea is not the answer, but it can be a way to the answer. If you are not first a master of yourself, then you are a master of nothing. The true tea master knows you do not need tea to access your own divinity. The way of tea is about cultivating certain virtues, skills, and noble attributes, all of the time, not just when we're having tea.

X

BEFRIENDING TEA

We may partake of tea for our personal enjoyment but she may have her own plans for us, her own agenda.

THERE'S A STORY of a man who ventured to South America to study herbs with a famous shaman. He followed him into the jungle with his notebook and began scribbling down the curative properties of each plant pointed out. But this man soon realized the shaman did not use herbs in this way. Instead, the shaman invoked the deva of the plant, the spirit of the plant itself. He called upon the plant to instruct him how to best utilize the plant for a particular malady. In our culture, herbalists prescribe certain plants for certain ailments but in the shamanic world, where plants are believed to be sentient beings, a plant may "advise" the physician. The people who started the Findhorn garden in Scotland were intimate with this dynamic. They had incredible success raising fruits and vegetables in a hostile environment because of their knowledge of and engagement with realms of the devas.

In his book *Plant Spirit Medicine*, Eliot Cowan writes: "If you want to actually use a plant yourself, the spirit of the plant must come to you in your dreams. If the spirit of the plant tells you how to prepare it and what it will cure, you can use it. Otherwise, it won't work for you.... There is only one active ingredient in plant medicines—friendship."

Cultivating a friendship with anything is a process of reciprocity. If neither partner feeds or nurtures the other in some way, the relationship will fall apart. Each has to contribute something. I have found it to be the same with tea.

As a young man I did not know that I could engage in a relationship with a plant. But as I grew older I realized that it doesn't take shamanic training to show your love and appreciation for any living organism. The book *The Secret Life of Plants* documented that plants not only have feelings but are sentient beings. I had forgotten this. The more I shared what I came to call my "Puerh epiphany," especially with gardeners, the more I was advised to explore that experience, go deeper with it, and make my own gestures of love and thanksgiving to tea. The results were amazing. I didn't have just one epiphany; I had many.

It all begins by creating a ritual space. This is a space of peace and stillness, of beauty, both within my heart and on my countertop. As I said before, creating this space can be as simple as taking a few moments to clear my mind.

Then, into this space I invite tea. I invoke the spirit of the leaf, the devas of the plant, and the soul of the species. When I pour water into an open saucepan, I say a prayer of thanks to the spirits of the water. When I light the stove, I ask that the spirit of the wind stir the flames of the fire. I ask the spirits of the fire to help boil the water, and then I turn my attention back to the water spirits, enlisting their help to make a decent cup of tea. As I wait for the water to boil, I acknowledge all the people that worked so hard to get these leaves to me. I also thank the soil, the rain, and the sun. I thank China, and I thank the tea. While the leaves brew, I place my hands over them, pouring out my love to bless them. When the tea is ready, I offer the first sip to my teacher and to the earth. What it's all about is being present.

There are many allies from the plant kingdom that we can engage for guidance and support. Tea is just one of them. They are carriers of wisdom for the planet, for hidden within the leaf may be glimpsed the moment of their creation. As an old Islamic saying goes, "The secret keeps itself."

Tea has been a tremendous boon to my existence. "The cup that cheers" and "dispelleth lassitude" has lifted my spirits time and time again.

Tea has also aided me in my struggle with sleep apnea. Theophyline and theobromine, both bronchial dilators, have, along with caffeine, encouraged me to breathe better, deeper.

The most dramatic "healing" has been more subtle. Tea has given me something positive and creative to think about during the day. It has "in-spired" me in more ways than one. Every hobby and interest I've ever had has come alive in tea: health and healing; botany and chemistry; mythology, spirituality and religion; and literature, poetry, art, and music. I am always learning something from tea. It is her nature as a teacher, and mine as a student.

Sometimes tea is only what you bring to her. The peace and clarity tea has afforded me these many years are partially the result of the love and devotion I have poured back into her. As I said before, you cannot approach her empty handed and expect her to respond. She feels our intentions.

The richest moments of tea time come long after the tea is gone, when I sit alone in silence, feel my heart open, and yield to the many stories she has to tell. It is in these moments of surrender that I am reminded of my place in the universe.

There are many ways to broaden your understanding and appreciation of tea besides making it for yourself. When you wade out among the bushes, brew tea with the local water, and partake of it in its own native hills with the people who grow it, your relationship with tea changes forever. A kinship, a bond, develops where one may not have existed before. But you don't have to go anywhere. If you want to get to know tea, grow it. Grow it from seed or nursery plants. Grow it in a pot. Grow it in your yard. Watch it flower, set fruit, and seed out. Make your own tea from the leaves. Make a Bach flower remedy from the blossoms.

You can even bathe in it. Take the waters. Immerse yourself in a pound of your favorite tea.

Tea is the "thunder in the middle of the lake," an arousing, mobilizing force of joy, whether we are inspired to dance out our hexagrams on the living room floor or rejoice quietly in our hearts. As tea is rooted in the earth, so are we rooted in this ancient tree. A tree from Central China. A tree from the center of the earth. A tree whose name means Great Goddess of Light. Thea! We sip the golden elixir that gives us breath. Her tresses, the tea leaves, are our sustenance, and from her breast we draw wisdom and life.

In thea sapientia.

In tea there is great wisdom and discernment.

茶道

XI

MASTER LI

LI AWAKENED with a start. His bedclothes were soaked. He felt a light breeze leaving through his pores, even heard it, and knew at once what it was. Exhilaration filled him, and then grief. I have an hour or two more to live, he thought. Time enough for tea.

Li had reverently performed all the ablutions and abeyances the night before, all the cleansing and censing that tradition obliged him to perform. So now he rose from his pallet, shuffled out to the front porch, sat down in an old wooden chair, and closed his eyes. There was no vitality left in him.

The wind shifted through the huge rhododendron trees towering above his house and a few floating lights from the devic world withdrew back into the woods. He stood and walked slowly out behind his house to a woodshed. In these predawn hours the dew had already come and his slippers became cold and damp.

He rummaged around in a few old burlap bags. "Here it is!" he said, and he reached both hands in and pulled out a black chunky material. It was charcoal he had crafted as a young man some fifty years before.

Li had not made this charcoal in the traditional way, but then he wasn't a traditional man. He had made this charcoal out of a tree he had known as a boy. The tree was his totem. It was one of "the wisdom trees" his family was responsible for.

He returned to his cabin and knelt down to place the charcoal in a stone brazier in the middle of the floor. It was still warm and aglow with coals from the night before. He brushed aside the old ash and placed his charcoal on the red-hot embers. It would take a while to catch. Time enough to gather the implements and utensils he would need for tea. It would also give him time to pray.

Master Li acknowledged the trees whose roots and branches he had cut to distill this charcoal. He thanked them for offering a part of their life. The trees had, in return, infused the wood with their blessing, giving back to this man a bit of the love that had helped to sustain them.

The night before, a student had brought Li a gallon of water he'd requested from a spring in the Six Tea Mountain district. It was water he knew well. There was a point on the brook, some ways along after it issued from the earth, where all five elements balanced and complemented each other.

He twirled off the lid of the gallon container, a glass mason jar, and sunk a wooden ladle in to the bottom.

"Water flows from high in the mountains. Water runs deep in the earth. Miraculously, water comes to us and sustains all life. Thank you, water!"

He extracted the ladle, raised it to his lips, and took a long draught. The moment he felt the cool water enter his mouth he recalled the many memories he had of this water as a young adult, for water has its own stories to tell, not only of itself but also of the rock that contains it. At its source, the water was tempered by its granite mother—cold, hard, obdurate. But some ways down the mountain it had softened, become more receptive. It had taken on a mix of minerals and nutrients, from the roots and soil through which it passed. It was this point along the creek where Li had made tea for his students many times.

It was this same water upon which the roots of the local tea bushes drew their sustenance, the same water that moistened the ground when it came as rain or dew.

He filled his stone kettle with this water and placed it on top of the coals. "I call upon the spirits of the wind to stir the flames of my fire. I call upon the spirits of the fire to boil my water and I call upon the spirits of the water to help make my tea."

He knelt on a pillow and pulled from the shadows a small tray. It was covered with a simple black silk cloth. He slid this tray along the floor until it rested directly between him and the heating kettle. He removed the cloth to reveal an earthenware teapot, two teacups, and a cloisonné caddy full of tea, all resting on a bamboo draining tray. He placed the tea caddy on the dirt floor to his side.

The tea he was going to use had been given to his great grandfather as a gift and was to be used by each member of the family only once.

The humidity of the room changed, and Li knew the water was ready.

He removed the lid of the teapot and placed it aside. Then, deftly, he lifted the heavy stone kettle and filled the teapot with water to warm it. He placed the kettle back on the coals and bowed.

He emptied the water from the pot into the cups, and when they warmed, he emptied the water from the cups onto the tray.

He then opened the caddy and placed some of the tea into the pot. It was a Pou Nei tea. He called it by its Cantonese name to honor his teacher who was from Guangdong. Its Mandarin name was Puerh.

Li lifted the stone kettle again and poured hot water onto the leaves. And here is where Li parted with tradition once again. Much to the dismay of his students Li did not pour off this initial rinse water. He simply didn't believe in it! He'd been to Xishuangbanna and seen how Puerh was made, but Li had his own way. He had been instructed by the trees of Six Tea Mountain (Luichashan) not to rinse. He told his students he didn't want to miss a single thing the tea had to offer.

He prayed: "Bless this tea and bless this water; may this union be made in heaven. I call upon the spirit of the leaf, the devas of the plant, and the soul of the species, to waken from your slumber and impart upon these waters the wisdom of the earth. And I shall endeavor to create within my heart a receptive vessel to receive this wisdom."

He prayed until the tea was ready, until he felt an inner prompting, and then decanted the tea into the two cups. One he raised in an offertory gesture to his teacher, Lu Tung Pin. When Master Lu entered the small room from the spirit world to receive his cup, Li felt the temperature in the room drop. He also felt the Fire of Tummo in his belly begin to flicker. The cup was taken from his hands. He bowed again.

Li then raised the second cup to his lips. He could smell the musty darkness of the tea, and then he tasted its woody depth. He followed the warm fluid down through his body and several moments later felt the warmth rise to his heart.

The room filled with light, and there was Master Lu, sitting opposite him, with whisk and sword.

And so Li passed over.

But Li did not leave his body through his crown. His last breath flowed out through the sleeves of his robe. And the folds of his garment shifted as in a light breeze.

Immortal Lu Tung Pin stood to receive his friend.

XII

AN INVITATION

SINCE I CANNOT make tea for you, as I would like, I invite you to find the spirit of tea for yourself. Choose your favorite tea, heat your water, warm your pot, and invite Thea to the table, too. When you are all settled down, here are some poems that transport me into that same luxurious space I enter when drinking tea.

While Visiting on the South Stream the Taoist Priest Ch'ang

Walking along a little path,
I find a footprint on the moss,
A white cloud low on a quiet lake,
Grasses that sweeten an idle door,
A pine grown greener with the rain,
A brook that comes from a mountain source
And, mingling with Truth among the flowers,
I have forgotten what to say.

—Lui Chang-Ch'ing

ON HEARING CHÜN THE BUDDHIST MONK FROM SHU PLAY HIS FLUTE

The monk from Shu with his green silk lute-case,
Walking west down O-mêi Mountain,
Has brought me by one touch of the strings
The breath of pines in a thousand valleys.
I hear him in the cleansing brook,
I hear him in the icy bells;
And I feel no change though the mountain darkens
And cloudy autumn heaps the sky.

—Li Po

A BUDDHIST RETREAT BEHIND BROKEN MOUNTAIN TEMPLE

In the pure morning, near the old temple,
Where early sunlight points the treetops,
My path has wound, through a sheltered hollow
Of boughs and flowers, to a Buddhist retreat.
Here the birds are alive with mountain light
And the mind of man touches peace in a pool
And a thousand sounds are quieted
By the breathing of a temple bell.

—Ch'ang Chien

The temple bell stops
But the sound keeps coming
Out of the flowers.

—Basho

SELECTED BIBLIOGRAPHY

American Camellia Society Yearbook. Fort Valley, GA: American Camellia Society, 1978.

Bin Fan Chen and Hong Sang Chan. *Science and Culture of Tea*. New York: Walt Whitman Publishing Co., Ltd., 1999.

Blofeld, John. *The Chinese Art of Tea*. London: George Allen and Unwin Publishers Ltd., 1985.

Bynner, Witter, and Kiang Kang-Hu. *The Jade Mountain: A Chinese Anthology*. New York: Alfred Knopf, 1929.

Chow, Kit, and Ione Kramer. *All the Tea in China*. San Francisco: China Books and Periodicals, Inc., 1990.

Cowan, Elliot. *Plant Spirit Medicine: The Healing Power of Plants*. Columbus, NC: Blue Water Publishing, 1995.

Emoto, Masaru. *The Hidden Messages in Water*. New York: Atria Books, 2001.

Evans, John C. Tea in China: *A History of China's National Drink*.

New York: Greenwood Press, 1992.

Gardella, Robert. *Harvesting Mountains: Fujian and the China Tea Trade, 1757-1937*. Berkeley, CA: University of California Press, 1994.

Gustafson, Helen, and Mark Gagnon. *The Agony of the Leaves: The Ecstasy of My Life with Tea* New York: Henry Holt & Co., 1996.

Hobhouse, Henry. *Seeds of Change: Five Plants That Transformed Mankind*. New York: Harper and Row Publishers, 1986.

Hohenegger, Beatrice. *Liquid Jade: The Story of Tea From East to West*. New York: St. Martin's Press, 2006.

Karcher, Stephen. *Total I Ching: Myths for Change*. London: Time Warner Paperbacks, 2003.

Ling, Tiong-hung, and Nancy T. Ling. *What's in a Cup of Tea*. Houston, TX: Yellow Emperor Books, 2003.

Lu Yu. *The Classic of Tea*. Translated by Francis Ross Carpenter. Boston: Little, Brown & Co., 1974.

Macfarlane, Alan, and Iris Macfarlane. *The Empire of Tea*. Woodstock, NY: Overlook Press, 2004.

Moore, Harry Thornton. *The Intelligent Heart: The Story of D.H. Lawrence*. London: Penguin Books, 1960.

Moxham, Roy. *Tea: Addiction, Exploitation, and Empire*. New York: Carroll and Graf Publishers, 2004.

Pratt, James Norwood. *The Tea Lover's Treasury*. San Ramon, CA: 101 Productions, 1982.

———. *The New Tea Lover's Treasury*. San Francisco: Publishing

Technology Associates, 1999.

Pratt, James Norwood, with Diana Rosen. *The Tea Lover's Companion*. New York: Birch Lane Press, 1996.

Proust, Marcel. *Remembrance of Things Past, Volume 1: Swann's Way and Within a Budding Grove*. New York: Random House, 1981.

Repplier, Agnes. *To Think of Tea*. Boston: Houghton Mifflin Co., 1932.

Rilke, Rainer Maria. *Letters to a Young Poet*. New York: Norton, 1954.

Sen Soshitsu. *The Japanese Way of Tea: From Its Origin in China to Sen Rikyu*. Translated by V. Dixon Morris. Honolulu: University of Hawaii Press, 1998.

Stoddard, Alexandra. *Tea Celebrations: A Way To Serenity. New* York: William Morrow & Co. 1994.

Ukers, William H. *All About Tea*. Reprint Volumes I & II. Westport, CT: Hyperion Press, 1999.

Wang Ling. *Chinese Tea Culture: The Origin of Tea Drinking*. Beijing: Foreign Languages Press, 2000.

Weinberg, Bennett Alan, and Bonnie K. Bealer. *The World of Caffeine: The Science and Culture of the World's Most Popular Drug*. London: Routledge, 2002.

Wilhelm, Richard, and Cary F. Baynes, trans. *The I Ching or Book of Changes*. Bollingen Series XIX. Princeton, NJ: Princeton University Press, 1950.

Wong, Eva, trans. *Seven Taoist Masters: A Folk Novel of China*. Boston: Shambala, 1990.

INDEX